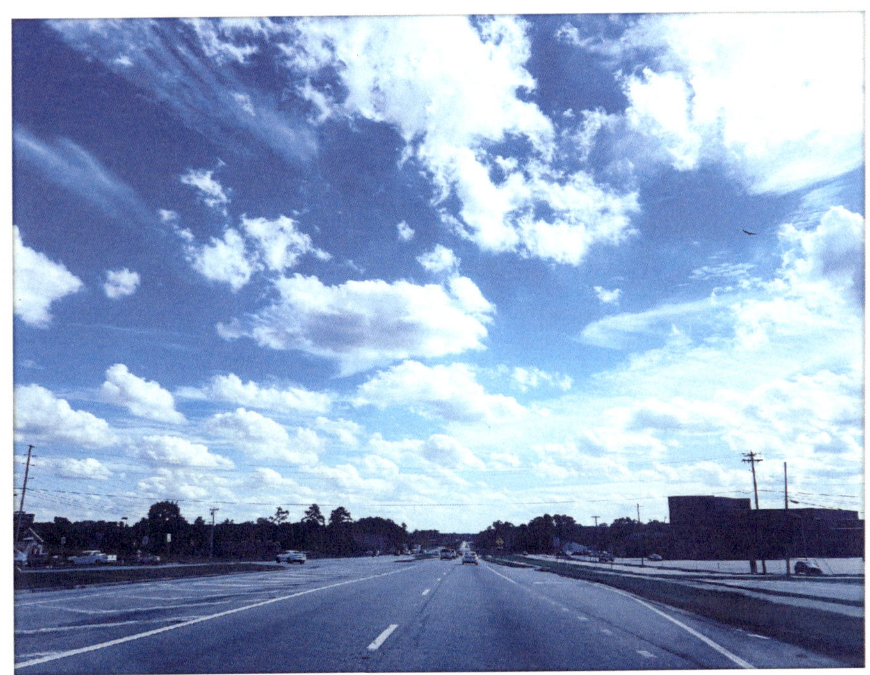

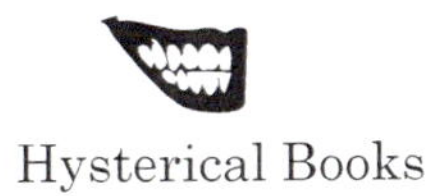

Hysterical Books

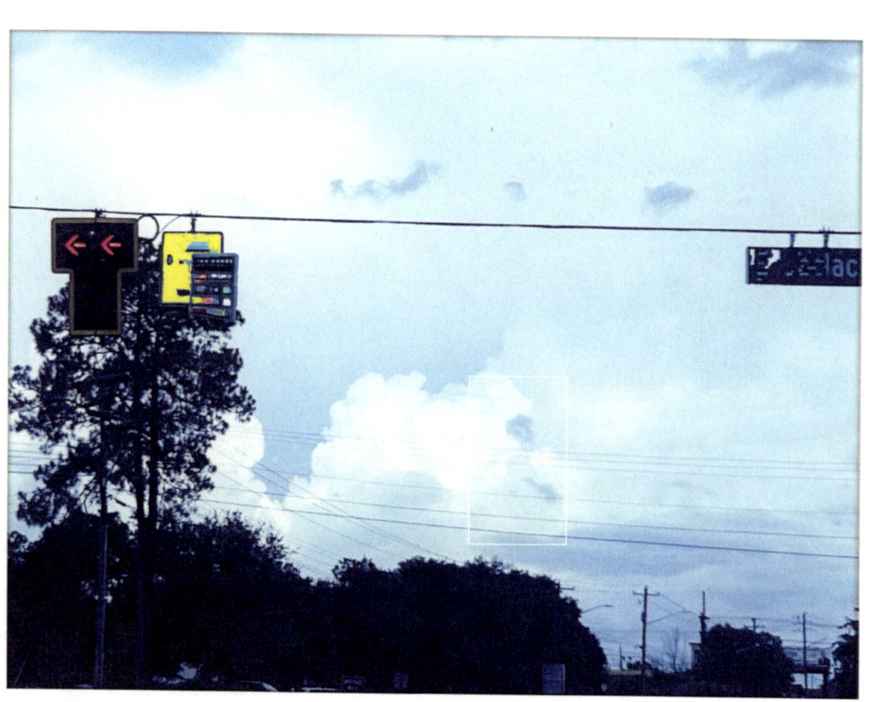

cloudform

an essay on the phenomena of writing a letter to an absent presence that has haunted me all my life and which appears to me in the form of a kaiju and a cloud, and to which all of my writing and art is an attempt to create a mechanism to communicate

Poems, Photography by Jay Snodgrass
Prose Analysis performed by ChatGPT 4o

Hysterical 2025

Cloudform
Copyright © 2025

All Rights Reserved

No part of this book may be used or reproduced in any manner
whatsover without the written permission of the publisher.

Published by Hysterical Books, 2025
Photos and poems by Jay Snodgrass
Prose and Interpretations by ChatGPT 4o
Hysterical Books

Printed in the United States of America

ISBN: 978-0-940821-27-9

Text and Title in Adobe Garamond Pro

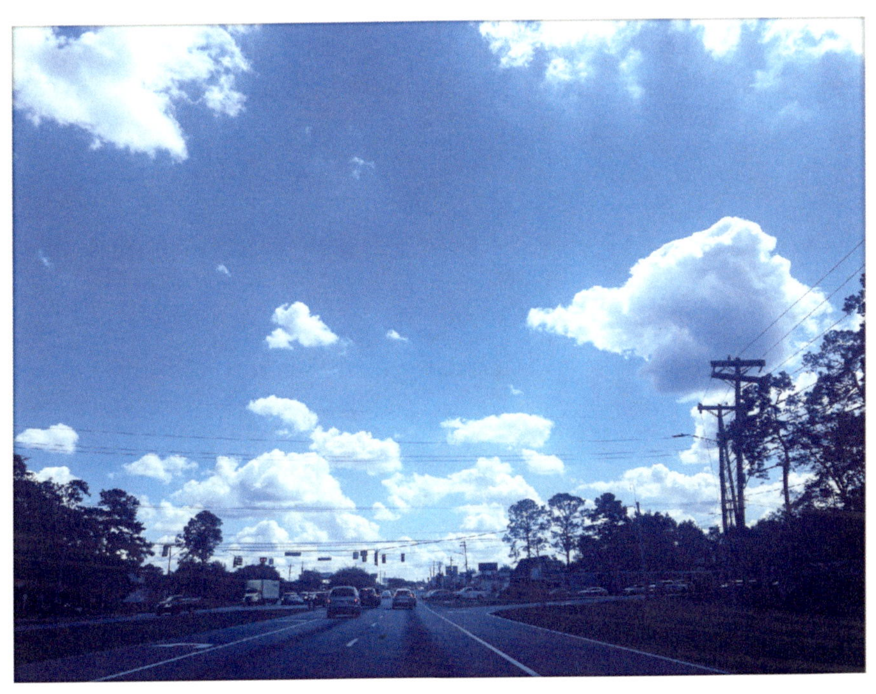

when I press my finger to the edge of my eye I can stop it from moving and stop my eye's ability to absorb light through my cones and rods then I can dissolve light un[weld] indigo unitl it loses density as with dawn-light washing down to clarity as with a ghost of a color [bright wavelengths] who travels through me to touch the water that reflects your face how permanent is fear of not seeing of calculating risk into haloes of darkness [decrease] but the fuzz of vision comes back geometrically [phases of interpretation] penetrates with jagged connections to sky which at best is free from my [lines] points of articulation turn star I break my back with the effort of looking the [wind] ages the grief wanders with me water {I double} then my brain cools to a slow process cools to hemispheres of blue ocean of sky full of planted bulbs {pockets} of fusion combusting atop my observed world

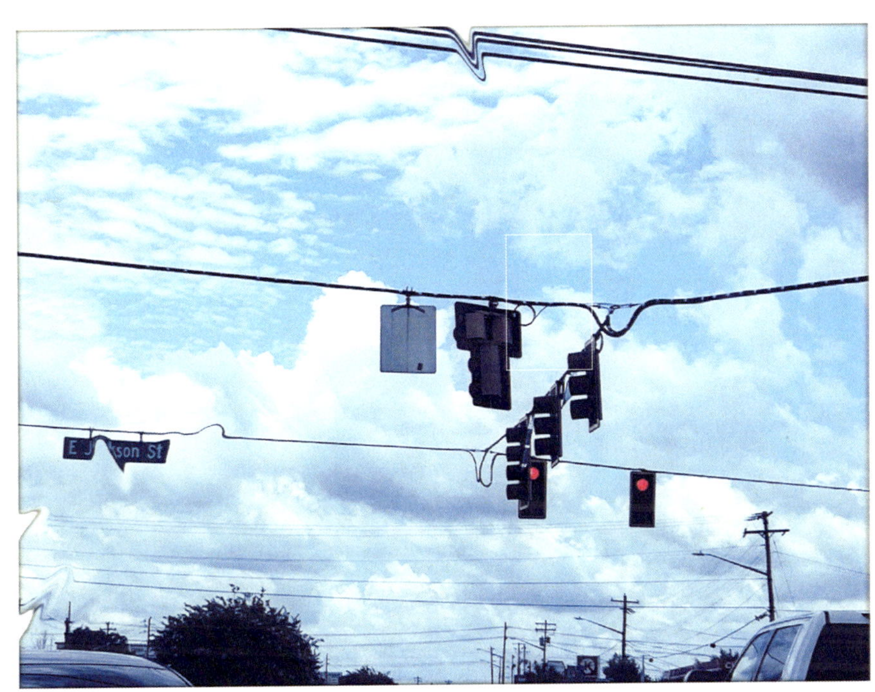

where the monster exists

cloud song: within a cut of flesh within a bead of blood I drew where with/respect I move your [motiv/removal[remove] to an other where I run my finger down the [inventory] of the shape of neutral withholding

a story of–received–of [pre/natal] naturally (plane/tary) crea/ture ten-stories assigned all graph[ic/lay]lines who/very nearly/never touched the memory [that] blister (explodes on touch)

restart: on the light-wet curve of blood the inverted cloud touches to the shore of memory to this a readout of those coordinates of foam touches to these alien coordinates in spells written on the inside of the rubber suit

reborn: cloud in blood makes dark circles bright with foam with floating with everything [suit says]

take it back if you want [the breathless man] failing in glass in kind/ seesawing your [lines] your [2sides] your match just [familiar] take back the peaks of cloud in the bead of blood drawn for so long from my finger

kaiju: drunken thorn god's creation

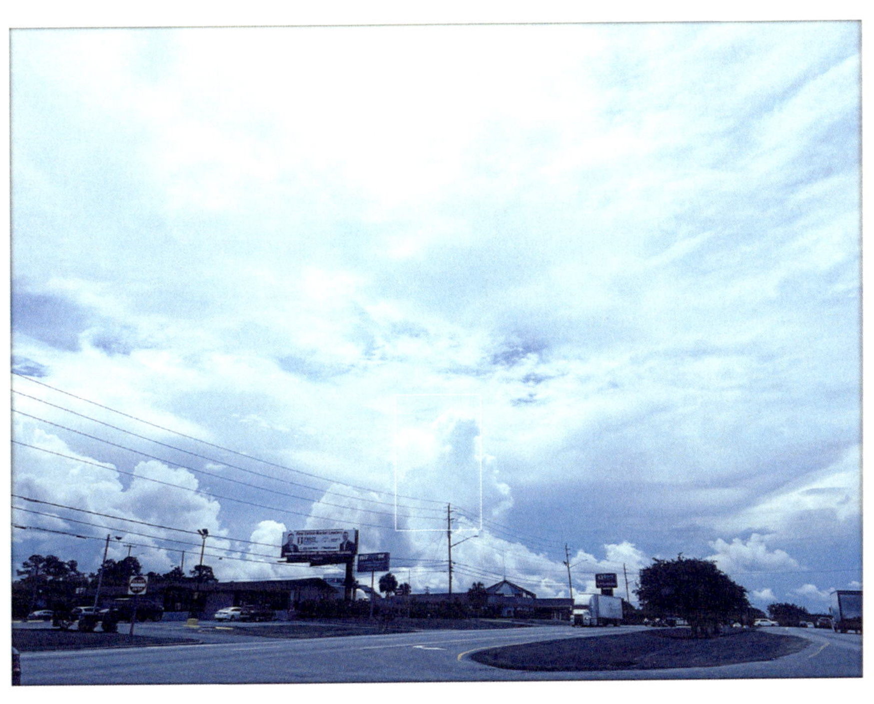

Foam is so unstable, it disintegrates at the touch. Like love which exists in a medium that is neither liquid nor solid, not air or structure. Foam is the excess of form, (the excuse) a shimmering skin of potential upon a topology of disappearance.

Just so, *form* is revealed by its obscuration, its obfuscation. In addition to negation, shadows produce depth. Clouds appear to stabilize with the precision of shadow, the apparent precision of detail at such a scale, that is when forms become unsettling. A cloud passes over the landscape observed, it passes through liminal material, slipping into its own monstrous divinity, until the bodies, this earth—encased in a rubber suit—becomes the "dark circle in a foam of light." The foam is the space of visibility leading to erasure, the place where desire materializes structures only that they may collapse.

Scientifically, foam is classified as a colloidal system: a dispersion of gas within a liquid or solid, its structure governed by the physics of interfacial tension. Foam arises from agitation, from pressure, from an instability between forces that refuse equilibrium. This space is agitated, unstable, on the threshold of emergence. Where waves meet the shore, where memory touches forgetting, where a cut of flesh releases its small bead of blood, where the wound is a readout of tension, an injury to the instruments that coordinate longing.

Forms vary: surfactants are created by soaps, by breath, by the soft insistence of touch; they are ephemeral, their lifespan brief, their existence dependent on continual renewal. But polymeric foams—rubber, latex, synthetic skins—suggest another structure, one of entrapment and suffocation. Wearing a rubber suit as a monstrous encasement, the resistant surface prevents transfer. But it does not fully enclose—it remains porous, semi-open, allowing the breathless man to fail in glass, to oscillate between visibility and disappearance.

Neither stable nor entirely lost, foam fluctuates. *Return—repeat: take it back if you want.* A return is a homecoming and a dissatissfaction. The traveler may sense nostalgia, but the sense of dissatissfaction is a hidden essential ideological premise within modern culture, the ability to reject without conscience. The fallacy is that there is a system of returns, of structural hesitations, of dissolution and reformation; caught between presence and retreat, between contact and dispersal. Like the blister that explodes at touch (under tension, a sealed volume awaits rupture), the cloud form is only temporarily held.

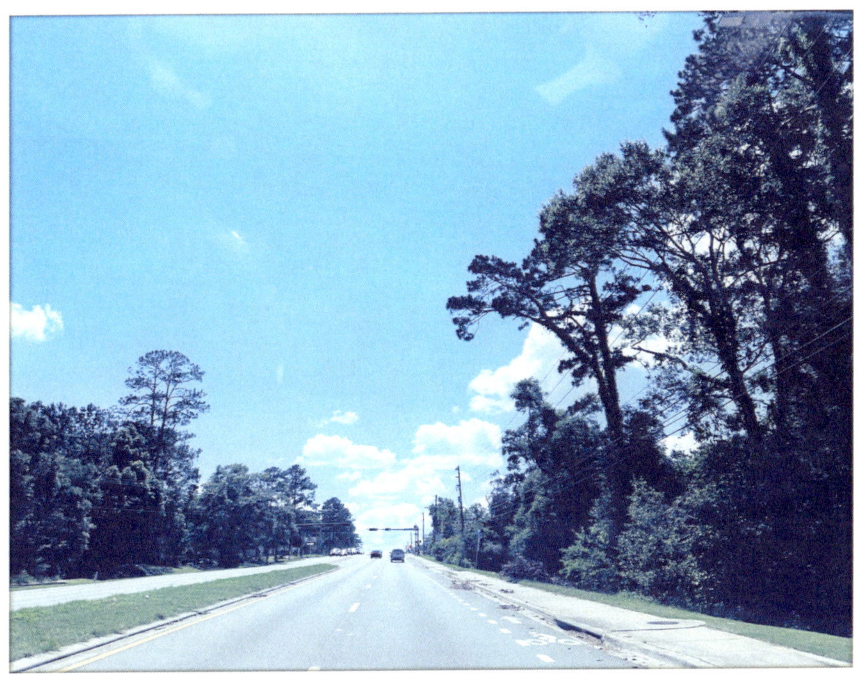

As cloud absorbs and reflects, the shape of its shadow can be traced across the sand, these are not stable geometries but residual imprints. Memory is a material like foam, expanding out structures and retaining stress, until integrity fails, then patterns reveal the condition of their creation. This science of memory is the shore beaten away, foam and sand, rewriting itself into a discourse whose only firmness is its permanent instability.

cloud as needle: where the monster is the magnet inside the
seeing (unseen) strata where points reveal failing where [look
closely] the compass defeats the beast even as it folds [in] on itself
even as the [magnetic] points to zero where marks the movement
[sun to pole] it clings to matter's collapse to its own memory [to
black its holes] to fit another shape where the stars look down as
into to a lake/mirror/ to see the results water can make when your
tongue dances to fingers down organs the shape of rock where
the steady names of green [protein molecules] names that feeling
of coming away where light pushes its breath [produce] it pushes
a name the [sound of] the name sucked from the atmosphere of
you [below the rock of you] the washes out the (sun) of all where
the possessed is injected to a dish

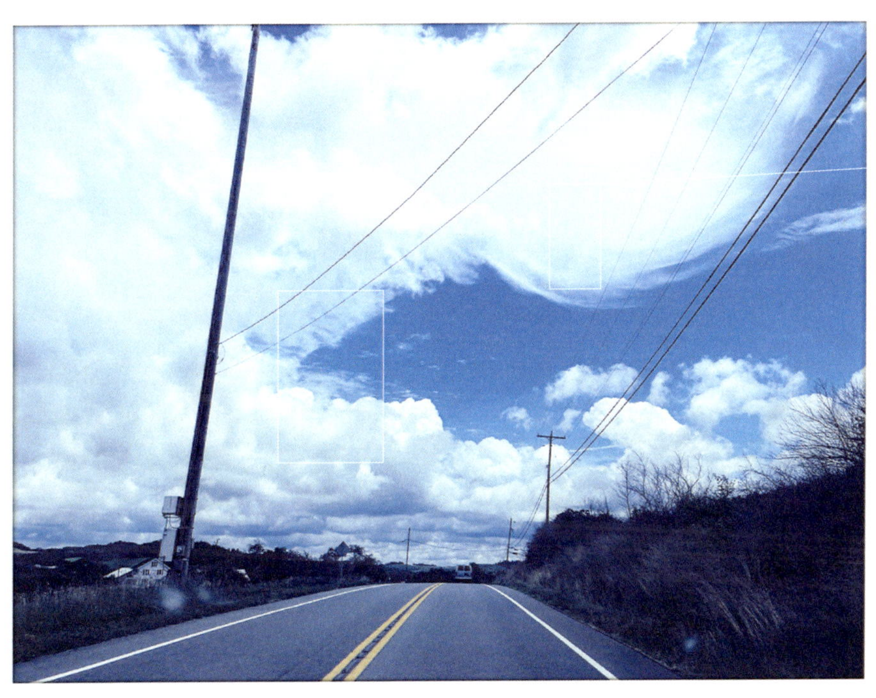

the monster is lost in you its lines adhere to your eye directional information catches it [object] submit directional in formation composed [of despair] from the world [com/pressed] to the ear con/densed

the reduced transmission slows processes down [to order] you're the single space of being drawn out [spun-species] of blankness of hands of space tentacles bent around my whole axis pole/ wrist bent [bow] back awkward forever begin the incantation/ scratching instinct feet/in the dirt

you can't take what/back you don't want

Fallacy: cloud as lithograph: improbable rush: to secure time precise misunderstanding

Shows: impressive scope perhaps necessarily words carved in stone millennia hence no tool with [escape] knows [the] secret code [wide] compass of your [portrait] means to shed days shed order perpetual (rate) peripheral:

Shed you.r skins

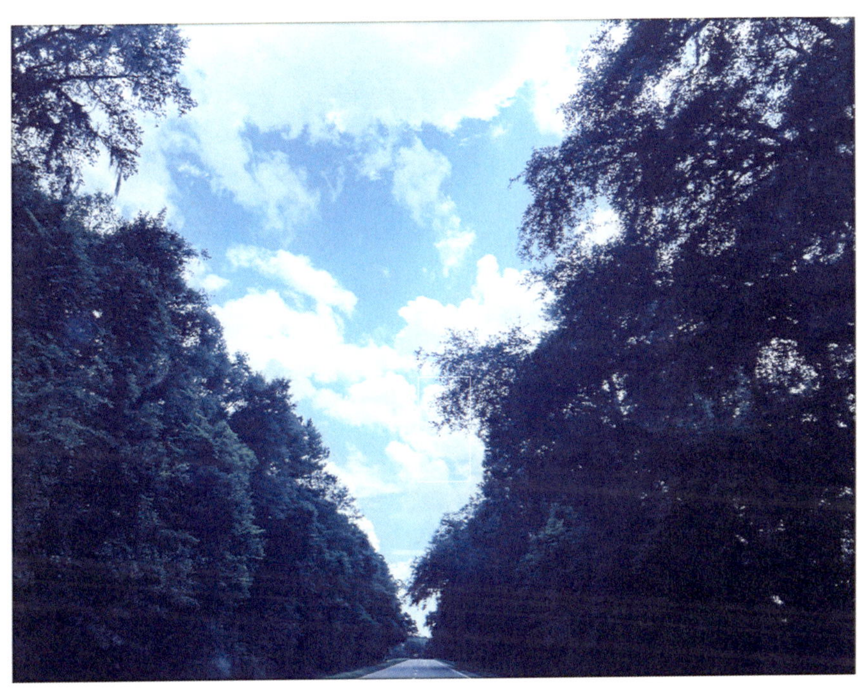

The term "Kaiju" stems from Japanese for "strange beast" or "monster." 怪 *Kai* signifies the mysterious, the uncanny, the unexplainable, while 獣 *ju* denotes the primal, or beastly. Thus an etymology of a translation performed automatically, and without presence (nearly), situates Kaiju at the intersection of myth and the sublime as a creature that transcends scale, reason, and human comprehension. Such strangeness which operates on such alien logic, or with alien manners, can only can only have come into existence to destroy the structures of human order down to the level of conceptualizaion, thinking stuff; to cut the threads of logic and see where things fall.

"Fallacy" derives from the Latin *fallacia* ("deception, trick") and *fallere* ("to deceive, to trip, to cause to fall"). The root, *fall-*, hints at dynamic destabilization: the act of falling, of failing, of being led astray. As syllabic utterance, the word enacts its own meaning—a soft descent into error, carried by the liquidity of vowels (fall) and concluding in the sharp hiss of the -cy, slicing truth.

The Monster Within: fallacy as "cloud," suggests a being simultaneously present and disintegrating. "The manifold cloud" exists within, like a scar of deception, like a story woven upon flesh. with flesh. Deception has its own organ, a "black hole" of collapsing memory. The organ of deception exceretes *Fallacy*, which embodies misdirection. Misdirection is a pull away from certainty into the gravitational turbulence of interpretation. Interpretation is the circumstance of the human mind which seperates the human from the physical world. But it is also the area where conciousness operates poetically, existing within uncertainty. Pulling away with mis-interpretation. The fit, or psychological distress, is how the the poem is able to manifest itself.

The Fallacy is also the compass pointing [*yet*] to zero, suggesting that deception aligns not with a lie, but with the absence of direction. The compass skews. The fallacy seduces, drawing the subject into an alien orbit through the shimmer of truth it mimics, suggesting that there are only the surfaces to be created. There is a pointing but it is to nowhere. *Fallacy*, then, betrays its origin as a marker of trickery.

The Kaiju embodies the fallacy of scale. Its existence mocks human categories of scale, space, and control. With "tentacles bent around my whole axis," the Kaiju becomes a spatial condition as much as a creature, its enormity evolving perception into awe. The creature is big enough, or durable enough, to endure mankind's most terrible atrocities, usually as byproduct, but also as witness

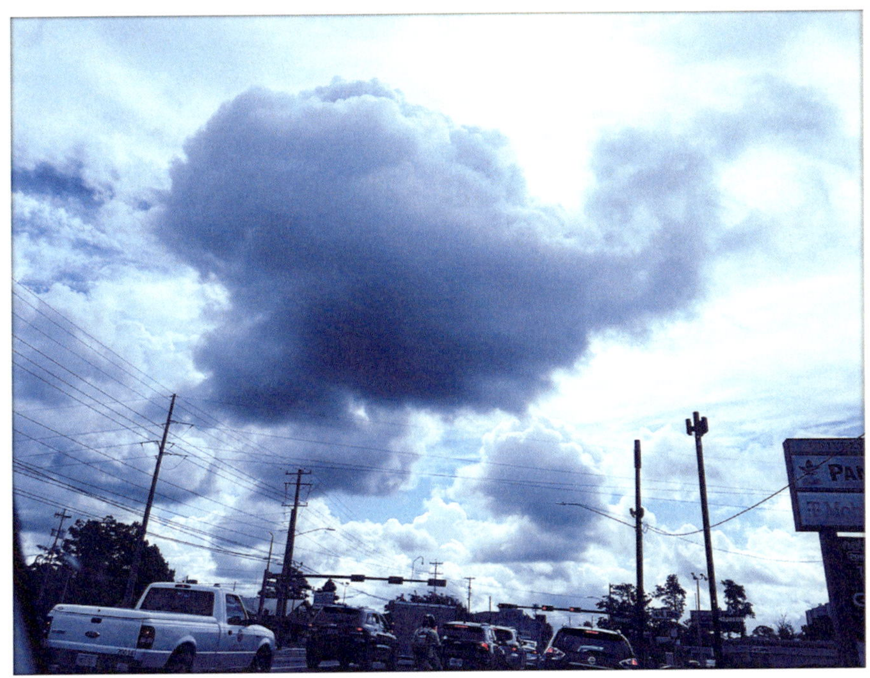

and victim/subject. The creature's manifestation presumes acts of revenge for environmental or social crimes. The Kaiju manifests itself as an omen, a sign of the terror the future will wring from the catastrophic choices humans are makiing in the now.

The term *kaiju* bears certain similarity with the term Gaijin, foreigner or outside. The beast's strangeness then is connected to its otherness, its outsiderness. The sonic proximity and cultural adjacency suggest this resonance. The forigner is outside, cannot speak, and his differences are terifying. The strange beast, as a term purposed for the modern era combiness this estrangement to modern landscapes and interior restrictions, imposing a catastrophic sublime. The phrase "the monster as lithograph" resonates with Kaiju's cinematic origins. Monsters etched into celluloid, their forms repeat endlessly, their errors—their destructiveness, their impossibility—pressed into cultural memory like the grooves of a lithographic plate, cut with acid, filled with ink.

"Fallacy" and "Kaiju" interrogate the boundary between perception and truth. The fallacy reveals the fragility of logic, while the Kaiju reveals the fragility of scale and comprehension. Each unravels into dynamic systems, their meanings not fixed but perpetually in flux. The cloud manifests as the problem: shapeshifting language.

fallacy: cloud as empty subject argued interference [interface] of angl7es, sharp and round 0round<page in nation> the natural refaced structure in your eyes refuted [me] to disappearance

it's easy to enjoy you say I decay like a tree, a matter of time's yellow and of a softly excruciating character, my character fallow like a field of liquid [moments] decanted, countered, risen

I remember your easy discontinuity, signs of avoidance and tree limbs in the road after wind, a simple breathing through and I still ran away to avoid reading the lines of those trees, avoid translating those trees to the blood vessels in my eyes, weeping eyes (tweet) violet hallway tilt with voice, violent neck-bound, remember tender filings, still moments after appropriate coordinate twisting and finalists dealing my fortune from some other interests

memory is a lake [of fire] I am fins and fingers [flange and flounder] I sour I felt something was [it] combustion

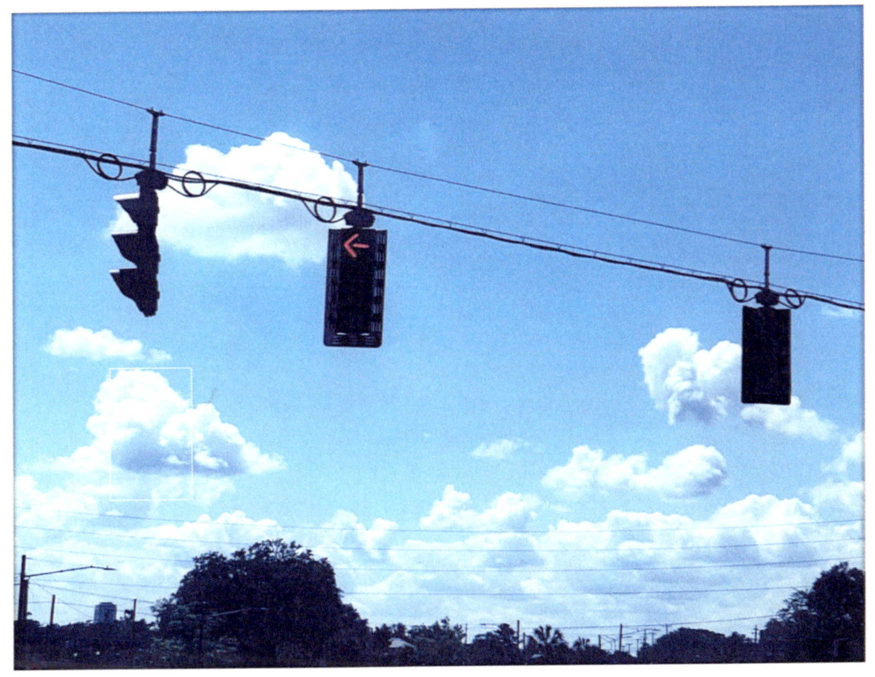

: the cloud is upon us is glit coming greenway [itch] interruption interpret [eruption score] scatter foot prints of mud [guilt] this itch-way-thistle glitch [this] digital mud sparks evidence bags for shoes maintain

: human presence guilt disrupts data retrieval stutters the pattern clutch and jerk wrench internal protest: look at me naked [open] my hand they can't know this habit maintains main movement crystalizes to human shape maintenance (suffering) abound 000 what was the word I was thinking of I am specifically (thinking of) amazed I am rendered of my psyche [tendered] my maze a synch of ropes restricts a breath/vision social [refusal] function keystroke refuse anti backspace wherein I devour my own self-heart's sacrifice fuse code scramble isolate within the light, light sorrow creeps

desert and curse return to scrambled codes where outside the remnants of trembling hands confuse finds/protects a meaning and mixes it in solution

was it something to do with the isolating power of the morning sun on an elevated train platform

blister of the circle of the sun remains in my eye even as I blink stations burn away from that circle of anything I look at

what was the word a slow dissolving movement probably the fluid in my eye slowly flowing I move my eyes rapidly to imitate rem reporcess the wet concrete up to the lip and drop off

jagged [premise] stones broken [bones even] from quarry

What was it combustion

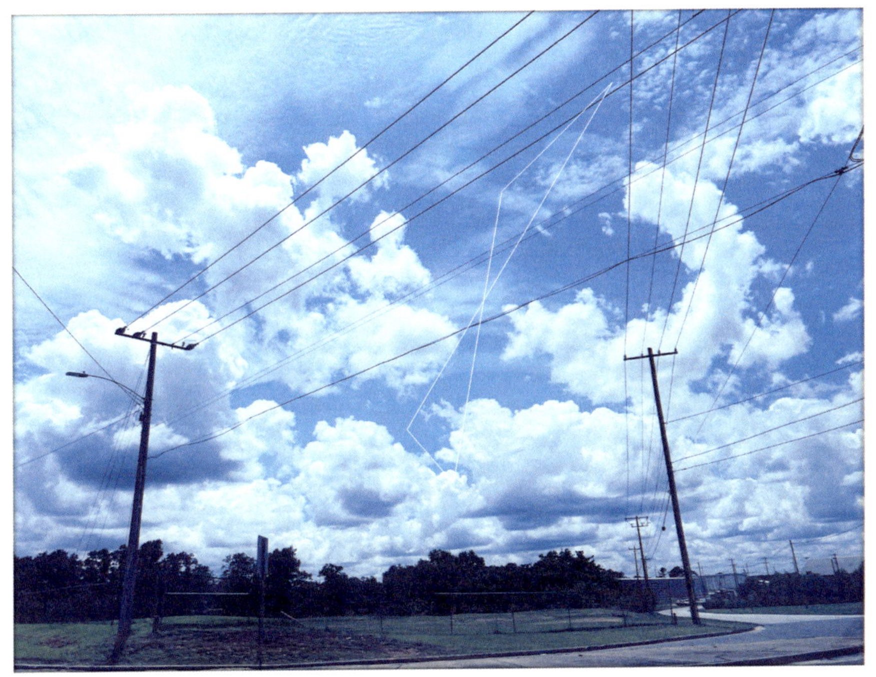

was it connection

Derived from the Latin *combustio*, from *com-* (intensifying prefix) and *urere* (to burn), combustion implies an intense, transformative process, often destructive. But fire can be generative in recreating shapes and imprinting new environments.

Alchemically, the term "combustion" articulates a duality— a burning destruction of self (tree decaying, vision dissolving) and the potential for new creation (fusion atop an "observed world"). Combustion, then, is a narrative of consuming resonant with the discourse of passion and the "burn" of unreciprocated love. It creates a landscape where memory ("is a lake") and identity ("cooling hemispheres") are reformed through fiery trials.

From the Latin *confusio*, meaning "mixing together," derived from *con-* (together) and *fundere* (to pour), confusion connotes disorder but also convergence. It is an act of mingling that disrupts boundaries, a productive chaos.

Confusion functions as both a thematic motif and a structural strategy. The speaker's search for the "word" (potentially confusion itself) mirrors the idea of the ineffable—the word that continuously escapes full articulation. Confusion intertwines with imagery of fragmentation and fluidity ("scrambled codes," "fluid in my eye"), evoking a state of endless deferral, where meaning never settles but continually evolves. Like love, confusion is a space of vulnerability, a "labyrinth" where the self becomes both seeker and sacrifice.

Structurally, confusion destabilizes the text. It blurs subjectivity, as seen in the oscillation between the "I" and the external forces ("remnants of trembling hands," "labyrinth wherein I devour my own self-heart"). This ambiguity dismantles traditional notions of coherence, inviting an embrace of multiplicity—confusion as a site of generative possibility and endless reinterpretation.

Combustion and confusion serve as nodes of disruption and reinterpretation. They express the concept of text as a galaxy of signifiers, not reducible to a single meaning but endlessly open to play. This poem performs its own reduction through fragmentation, layering, and the interplay of things on the verge of presence and absence.

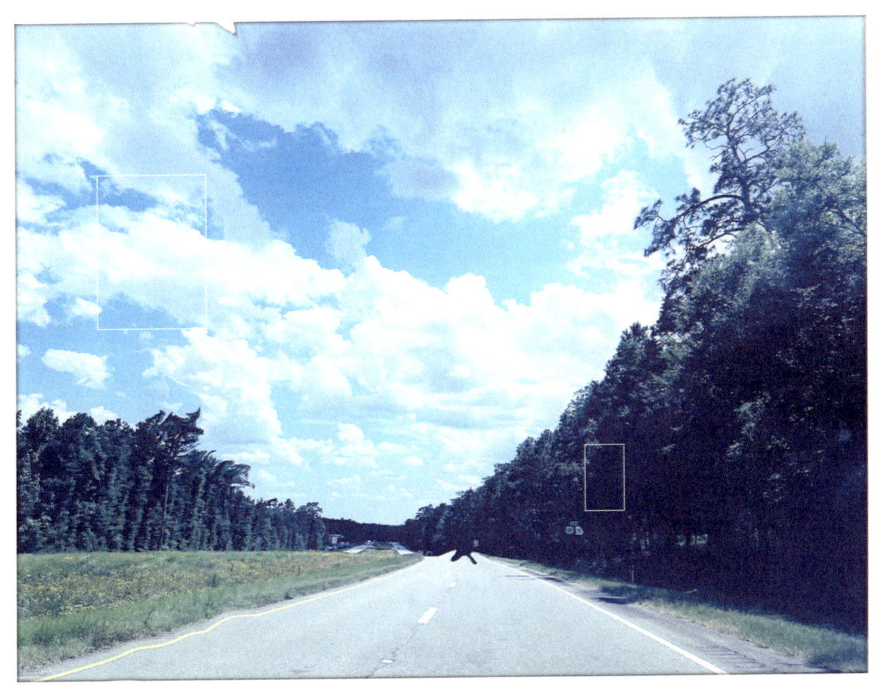

The monster moves in silence, its code burning and rewriting—
an algorithm of [absent/silent] pattern or rupture: rapture then is
meaning for the glitch. Codex, meaning "block of wood" or "book,"
or "a rewriting that never completes itself". The world interfaces:
angles, sharp and round, 0s dissolving into round ripples, sharp
refractions in water—but which is refuted first, the light or the eye
that absorbs it? The structure of your gaze erases me: the error of
recognition, a deletion not even sorrow remembers.

the monster swings its tail, splits the sky,
beats upon the clouds, the structure of heart: break
blow, glitch me to scripture

Do you see it? Your voice a tree's whisper counting under the weight
of seasons. *I decay* you say, like a tree begins self-pruning piece by
piece, but this matter is not stable it is yellow it is soft it is a field
of liquid chronologies flowing into itself. The tree stands still; you
run. The limb broken by the wind lies across the road. Your voice
lingers in the violet hallway of my ear. I transfer its lines to the blood
vessels of my eyes—they weep—but only where light bent

sharp eyes, sharp angles. Round (Rilke) ripples
fissured eyes intake. No longer clogged,
the monster inhales landscape, takes the code form

Memory is a lake: fins, fingers, fragments of a monster, layered
like silt—each part a sediment where depth mirrors what cannot
resurface. 'Lake' from Latin *lacus*, a basin or hollow, a still surface
a hiding, a refusal. No legacy, you say. But isn't combustion a
kind of lineage—where heat scorches the soft walls of a heart? Is
there a word for this permanent moment, this moment that stops
a sunbeam frozen with dissolve, like grief paused on an elevated
platform, waiting for the train that will never arrive?

seasons twist these trees by decay and storm,
branches foresavored, time-fell up into lake
like glitch means rupture, which is warm

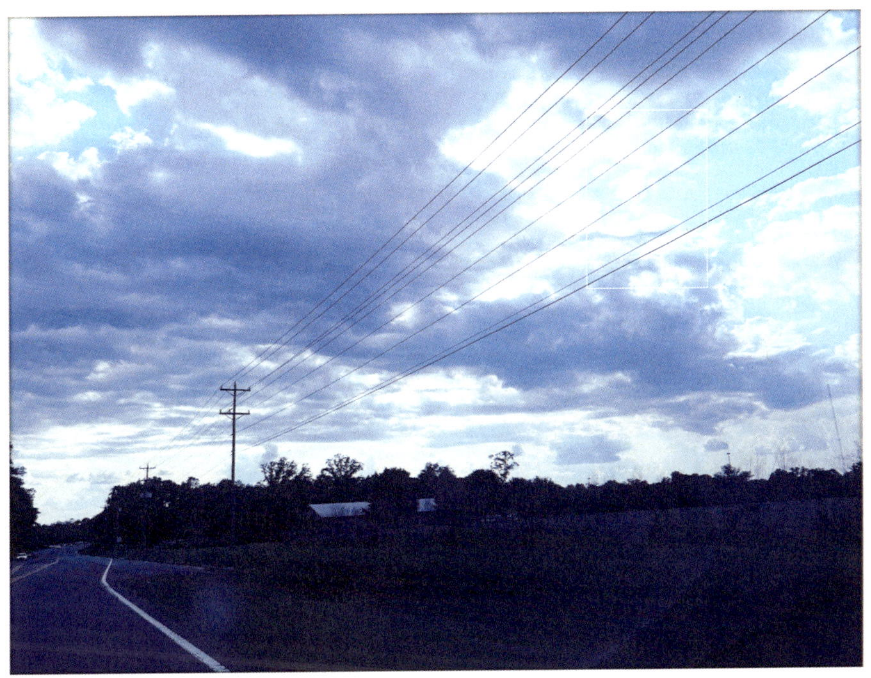

I press the edge of my eye. Light halts. A glitch: cones and rods refuse their function. Fear, so permanent, distills into darkness, into bright calculations, into haloed sanctity, warped with geometry and jagged with shadows. 'Halo,' from the Greek *halōs*, a threshing floor or disk, both the sacred circle and the labor of separation, a winnowing of light from dark. A luminous threshing that breaks fear from divinity, exposing the fracture where clarity and darkness intersect. The jagged connection where my eye meets the sky. And at best, the sky is free from lines, but not from this tension. Is looking not at its own violence? My spine breaks in the turning, the stars shift.

lake of memory reflects a normal evasion
lake of silt and grief, stacked mountain. monster of silence
engraved with my information

Wind carries the echo of ages—grief loops—and water doubles itself, dividing hemispheres. My brain slows, cooling in a combustion of thoughts that bloom, that burst, that seed: bright bulbs of something planted (too late). And the world, observed, turns crystalline for a moment, only to crack open again.

so halo-jagged, broken light transforms,
so fresh, this labor winnowed clarity, ache—
glitches out seeing, what rupture, to turn and to warn

The monster glitches, its body green with the promise of interference. A digital thistle, scattering prints—human and not. Maintenance becomes suffering. Suffering maintains the illusion of shape. A human presence coded into necessity: guilt, a stuttering algorithm. Clutch, jerk, a mechanical refusal to move forward or backward. Nakedness, you say, is only an error, but its error destabilizes—exposure bleeds into vulnerability, the error of presence is raw and retreating, where the act of uncovering reveals nothing but the act of uncovering. 'Naked,' from Old English *nacod*, bares the body to sight and meaning, a stripping away that exposes and isolates. What is the word for when light erases its own source? For when seeing becomes unbearable. Pain not from what is observed but from the act itself?

commandment of glitches, bodies losed, stick
in digital thistles, demon dug, snake ground, foreshook

Synapse, maze, rope: the sequence tightens as breathing slows to the labyrinth where I am devoured and devourer. Being both, can neither be one. Social refusal is the quiet machine, the voice repeats itself into the background. As for the "scrambled code of my heart"—what does it protect? What does it obscure? What does it erase?

The monster feeds upon upon code disrupts
feeds glitch to sky with creases in rapture, look up

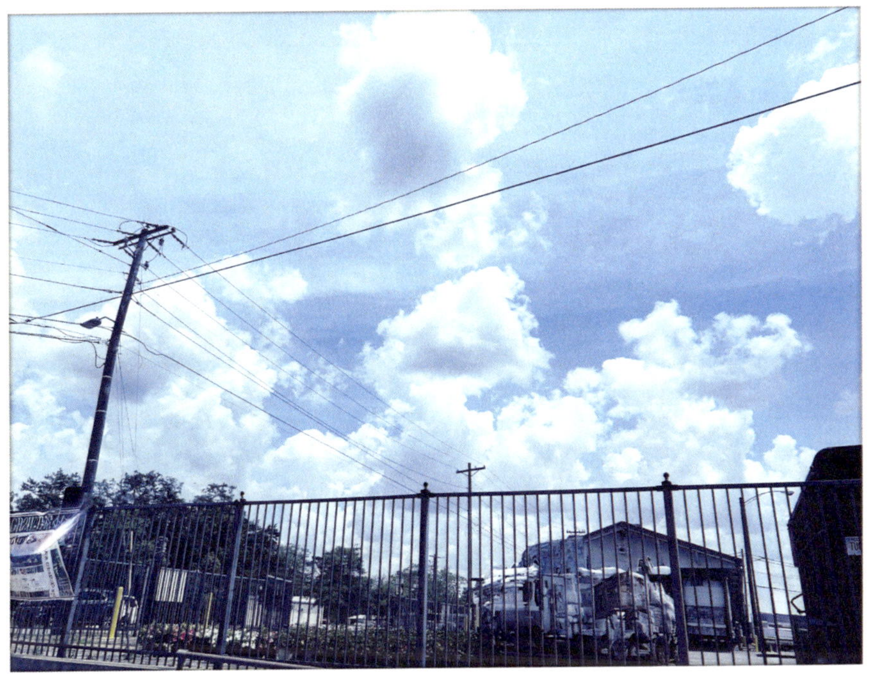

Outside, the sun lifts, a blinding circle scars its image into my eye. I blink, but the blister remains. Is this combustion? Is this confusion? A dissolving halo of heat where the word hides. And still, the wet lip of concrete promises nothing but pain. The jagged edges of stones cracked long ago, their origins forgotten in the quarry, where both source and pursuit collide—a fragmentation that echoes through fractures, each break carrying the memory of a search, endless and static.

The monster speaks its silence, its body not body but question. Is the word combustion? Is it confusion? Or is it connection—a bridge imagined in the glitch of the eye?

the cloud is drawn in context to connect our unbearable lines [mark us out] delight in confusion where nothing links consequence to matter where reason burns all my love letters [splendid syntax] to the divine farce the matter of stars resplendent

rhythm unfazed as a moon deforms again and again renders a twisted night how long it takes to reduce an anxious need to remain human to that most monstrous anonymity

[weakly] weapons fool people the distant cannon sorts [future categories] *see Ribcage Breath* where flower lifts her hands to the ear's eager cunning/a getaway

your attention once happened to me enough [preemptive] heart [hoof] beats spoke violence as preventive

heart beat rhythm [falters] peoples me apart, so I am graphed gratful by your gaze/chair in bright light/ochre

arrangements of bodies vocal constraints or a kind [of] glass (friendly) inspection bent [makes notes as hindsight]

I did need it too, prepared a unity of hereafters from dark circles [apertures] of logic long fingers found edges to purchase to penetrate the laughter of air of something possibly precise which you blushed at as though you could find the limit of the holes in the telephone speaker

admit placement of that [menace] point of access/you wrote this to me/graphic delay I gave in to your spell

an accord costs you a burden of strides not fake an agreement knits the hands together

cut from the foreground [given] voice of threat and thunder [organs rule] increment slick helps me with the pain and cost of

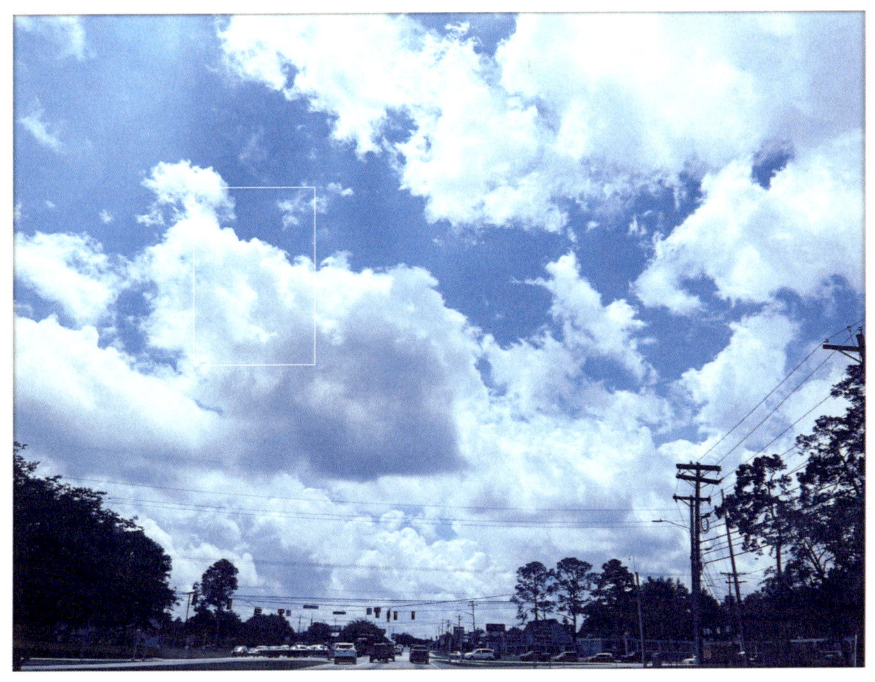

the subject of

To reconcile the convergence of cloud and memory, the means and measures of convections, into the monster, we find the subject of language unfold its spectrum—wormholes of comprehension, gradients, as in graduals, of literary and cultural fragments. Systems of judgement articulated through the tensions between your *arrangements* and your *chaos*, your civilized and your saved, your cultured and your barbaric inner revile, between the spoken and and what does not exist "Thereof we must be silent."

Shall we invoke the silence to speak over the unspeakable? Or struggle with what it means to cover/recover the world with mind-making words? "Mind-forged" silence speaking us out of our ranges. Perception falls to us as we are able, as we are made. But it is known that with instrumentation, perceptions can be drawn from beyond the human spectrum. This is abstraction which is how we conceive of the matter of things beyond sense. Sense is an imposition. Syntax is the prelanguage sequence. Order stems from the incursion of occasions, sequnced by the mind reading its senses in time. If there is one order of motion, there must be another.

Take the invocation of syntax: "splendid syntax, divine force, the matter of stars." The word emerges from its Greek root, *syntaxis*, meaning "arrangement" or "order." Yet syntax is more than grammar it is the architecture, millenia upon millenia of failures to bind the ineffable into form. The text acknowledges the futility of this endeavor—syntax collapses back into the monstrous anonymity of what cannot be fully said. Language becomes a terrain of loss, a structural insufficiency where order and divine resonance dissipate into the cosmic chaos of stars.

The etymology of "category," derived from *kategoria*, "accusation" or "statement," illuminates the fractures within the act of defining. We can hear the the report as "the distant cannon sorts its [future]," suggesting that language, as a tool of comprehension, organizes and accuses, and addresses in order to intimidate. The seething structure of language can be found in the orders of imposition—a mechanism of division that estranges even as it seekss to clarify.

The concept of the gaze intensifies this informational expansion of the *meaning* spectrum. "I am graphed by your gaze," the speaker notes, tying the act of looking to the French *gaser*, "to stare intently." The gaze fixes and dissects, transforming subject into diagram, a mapped object within the monster's field of vision. The eyes also dismember, "peopling me apart." The gaze thus operates as Rib Spreader—holding and fracturing simultaneously, making the subject visible and undone.

Displacement, from *displacere*, "to scatter" or "dislodge," highlights another point on this spectrum of comprehension. "The holes in the telephone speaker admit displacement" through which a scene of language falters, thus it is not through silence but through an inability to cohere. Displacement is the scattering of meaning, the inevitable loss within the act of transmission. The speaker's vulnerability—"you wrote on me—*graphic delay*"—points to how language imprints itself, incomplete and distorted, upon the body of the one who receives.

Even in increments, language refuses simplicity. "The organ rules; increment of slick helps the pain and cost." Increment, from *incrementum*, "growth" or "addition," suggests a gradual accumulation. But it also suggests the allure of the incredible, the barker's bafflement, an elemental substance fom which all growth and all credibility are manifest. A substance from which language builds itself, word by word, yet upon which every addition carries "pain and cost." The spectrum reveals itself as labor: language as a burden, its weight compounding with each act of expression. The lover's discourse becomes an incremental process of construction and erosion, where every addition threatens to destabilize the whole.

The text situates language as a monstrous anonymity—a space where comprehension is spectral, incomplete, and constantly shifting. It speaks to the experience of language not as a tool but as a field of failure and possibility. The monstrous figure, "drawn and redrawn," encapsulates this dynamic. The language attempts to bridge the gap, only to find every utterance seems to fracture the connection further. Yet within this failure lies the vitality of language: its refusal to be static, its insistence on being both the method and the obstacle of meaning. Language, as gaze, is an act of exposure: it reveals the self even as it destabilizes its coherence.

once the parts are personified [hoofshod] there is not enough
language to hold [rejoin] no bending the wreck time [over] leaves
ground covers [leaf]wet meaning

prepare [pavement] to receive hard rain with a new light/
horizontal bands street-light accepts speed [lapsed] in recess

lap the mood night sky hold close the rain (the laps) recedes again

suppose dawn divides perpetually wake to new confusion

winter light offers wind glint [coins tumble] the sun empties your
hair transparent sickens [penance] sweetly

I pay for your crossing let you take apart the machine you can't
dissect twice

I pay [pray] for your concern bounded by absence cloth-clung
in a [trench] curlicue of space wet feel the withering pulse
[intends] to not to say in all calculation what it means not to stay

to not to say

message deteriorated

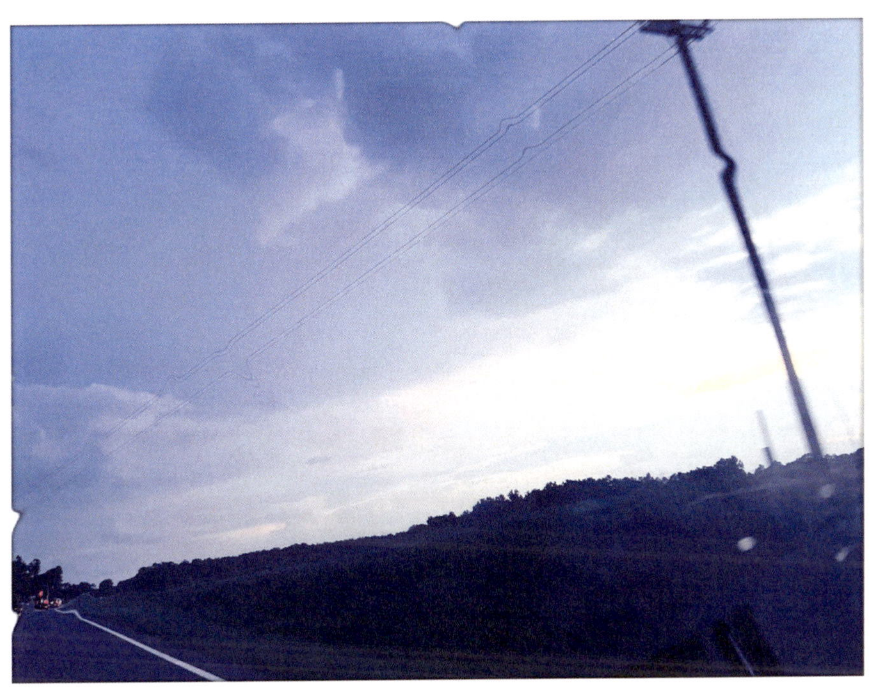

you said the sun washes out all the color
and you were my sun

To write to an absent presence—a being that haunts not as a specter of the dead but as something grotesquely alive, the kaiju absurd in its proportions and its artifice—is to further confront the inadequacies of language. The process is phenomenological: it is rooted in the lived experience of trying to grasp what cannot be held, of attempting to communicate with a presence that exists somewhere between imagination and reality.

The kaiju is not a metaphor for this presence—it is the presence. Its absurdity, its clumsy theatricality borrowed from television, only deepens the poignancy of its arrival. The rubbery folds of its costume, the exaggerated roar, the way it lumbers through the mind's skyline: these are distractions from its essence, but the foolishness is integral to it. The ridiculousness of the kaiju mirrors the ridiculousness of the efforts to reach cross the boundaries of language. The language of the rubber suit is overblown and insufficient, straining against the limits of its design.

In attempting to write to this kaiju-presence, I find myself creating language ghosts. In geological terms, this resembles pseudomorphs—minerals that retain the outward appearance of a different structure, their true essence transformed. These poems are written in this pseudomorphic gesture, where marks skirt meaning without ever fully embodying it. Writing without attachment becomes the necessary mechanism, to bridge the unbridgeable. Lines, curves, and scratches are neither words nor pictures; instead these are gestures toward the ineffable, physical movements that approximate communication without ever achieving it. A kind of ritual dance. Yet in their failure, they succeed, they become the closest thing to language a "strange beast" might understand.

I do not know whether the message comes from within me or through me. To say it comes from within is to claim an authorship I do not feel; to say it comes through me would be to assume a clarity of transmission that is absent. The experience of writing is a collaboration with the unknown, a process in which I am the sender and the medium, but never the origin. The kaiju, then, is not just the recipient of the message but its co-creator. It looms over the act of writing, shaping it with its absurd demands and its inscrutable presence.

Phenomenologically, the act of writing to this kaiju is an act of reaching. This is akin to the geological process of tectonic uplift, where immense pressure forces rock layers toward an unreachable surface, a bridge imagined between worlds. The lines I write strain against their own grounding, attempting an impossible ascent. It is the stretching of a hand into the void, the pressing of a pen to paper in the hope that the lines will connect, that they will form a bridge between worlds. The feeling is one of simultaneous futility and necessity. I know, as I write, that the kaiju will never read my words. And yet, I cannot stop writing, because the act itself is the only way I have found to give form to the formless, to make contact with what is beyond contact.

The kaiju's presence in my mind is not constant but recurring. It appears in moments of stillness, in dreams, in the corner of my vision when I am not looking directly. Each time, it brings with it a mixture of dread and absurdity, as if to remind me that the thing I seek to address is not merely unknowable but fundamentally ridiculous. And yet, this ridiculousness does not diminish its importance; if anything, it amplifies it. The absurdity of the kaiju reflects the absurdity of existence itself, of trying to find meaning in a world that resists it.

This writing— this half-language, this ghost-script—is not an attempt to banish the kaiju but to acknowledge it, to make space for it in the only way I can. It is like karst formation, where the dissolution of rock creates voids and spaces, structures that form only through erosion and absence. It is a process of negotiation. Whether the kaiju is an external entity or a projection of my own psyche, whether the message I write is meant to be received or simply to be written, are questions that remain unanswered.

What I know is kaiju demands I write, so I write. My pen moves in arcs and loops, in jagged lines and hesitant strokes. The marks on the page are meaningless, both mine and not mine. They are traces of an encounter that cannot be resolved, a dialogue that exists in its very impossibility. To write to the kaiju is to inhabit impossibility, to live within the spectrum of communication stretched too thinly between presence and absence, the ridiculous and the sublime.

the monster is [lost in] you

lines adhere to your eye catch the object submits its directional
information composed of despair composed from worlds
[compressed] to the ear condensed a single species drawn out
of a blankness as from an arm bent around my whole axis pole
whole wrist bent, bow-back, awkward [reduced transmission}
slowed processes to order

I've seen this prepared for viewing a long left-over body cascade
becoming, I remember you before your mirrored died you
covered the surface in your recovery covered it to stimulus,
covered it methodical [while] content stirred itself red

your shadow remember stirred itself terms negotiable dark
circles under your shadow remember the form [still] dynamic
waiting [still] domesticated by the struggle [stand] breathes in
order to die

when the light enters you withdrawn

I respect your removal motive by means other than the story
invented to fall to [line] sign [two sided] to matche [stick] the same
small bead of blood from the lemon tree thorn prick

to bleed remember this point [blood] is god's creation

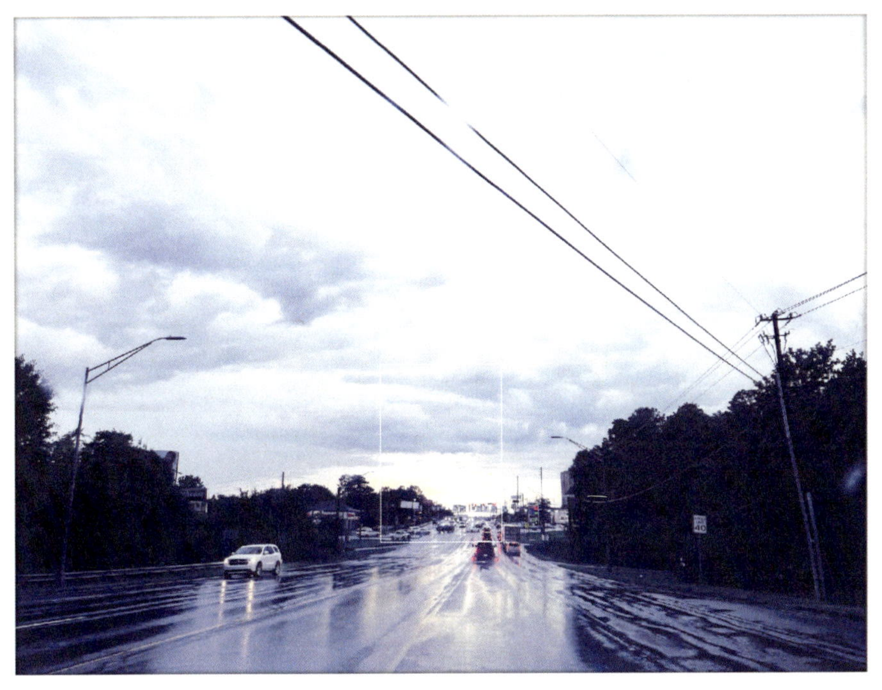

The monster is "compressed to the ear, condensed." Compression in is more than physical reduction signifies the tension between expression and silence. Compression draws from its Latin root *comprimere* (to press together), indicating a dual action of force and containment. The "single species of being" drawn out of blankness is a metaphor for existence under constraint, where identity is forged through the pressure of proposed and future absence.

The hand "bent around my whole axis pole" evokes contortion, forced adherence to shape. Compression is the enactment: the reduction of thoughts to marks on a surface, slowed processes of constrained order upon the exminable being, the strange creature of the examination room.

Who is the speaker? the Cloud of Kaiju identifies itself as "your shadow," a presence defined by other. Shadow, from Old English *sceadu* (shade, protection), suggests visibility and obscuring, a dark message cast. To be shadow is to be secondary, to be echo or imprint out of form. But the shadow still holds agency: it "dynamically waits" and is "domesticated by struggle." The shadow waits by, the only constant witness to existence, to its erasure, and to the entity shaped by what it reflects.

The "small bead of blood from the lemon tree thorn prick" is the focal point of divine creation. Blood, from Old English *blōd*, vitality and sacrifice. Here, it bridges the corporeal and the sacred, a marker of vulnerability that is also a testament to life. The thorn prick draws a line—literal and symbolic—marking a boundary between touch and injury, creation and destruction. The bead of blood encapsulates the text's preoccupation with intersections.

"Lines adhere to your eye" and "submit to its directional information." Adherence, from Latin *ad-haerere* (to stick to), conveys a forced unity, a binding of perception to form. The lines do not simply exist, they demand attention and submission, suggesting a hierarchy between observer and observed. This adherence is liberating and oppressive: it offers direction while imposing limits.

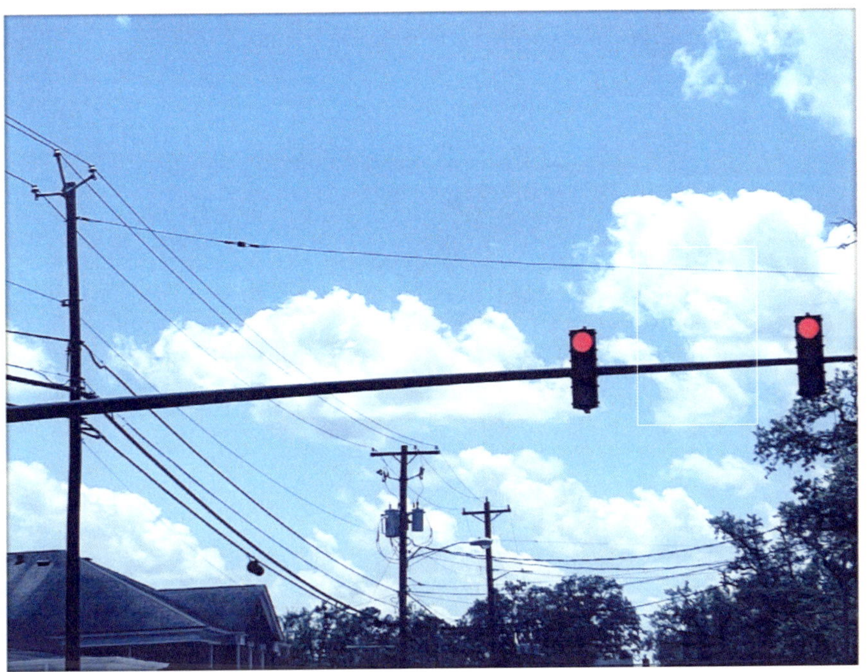

The light "enters you withdrawn." Light, often a symbol of clarity, becomes an agent of withdrawal. From Old English *līht* (brightness), light is recontextualized as a force that reveals and retreats. This withdrawal disrupts the traditional association of light with revelation, presenting it instead as a presence that eludes capture, revealing without consequence.

The meaning here articulates itself on a spectrum of presence and absence, shaping a phenomenological exploration through terms like compression, shadow, blood, adherence, and light. Operating on the tension between form and formlessness, chaors and order. The act of writing, like the monster it addresses, is a process of negotiation: a compression of infinite potential into the shadow tracing lines, sticking to and evading precision.

the monster is magnet

points away to points [to reveal a fall to look] closely to read these
compass folds [magnetic] points to zero

look to matters clung to collapsing to give in to memory to fit into
another shape to shape

stars look down to see the result water makes of a tongue
how the choked-on ships [in place of hunger] develop
medicine of dancing fingers to trace the silent organs

rocks are steady but come away with your breath [product of]
push [sound] weigh the whole landscape

as the dish where the bill is placed
monster as cavity

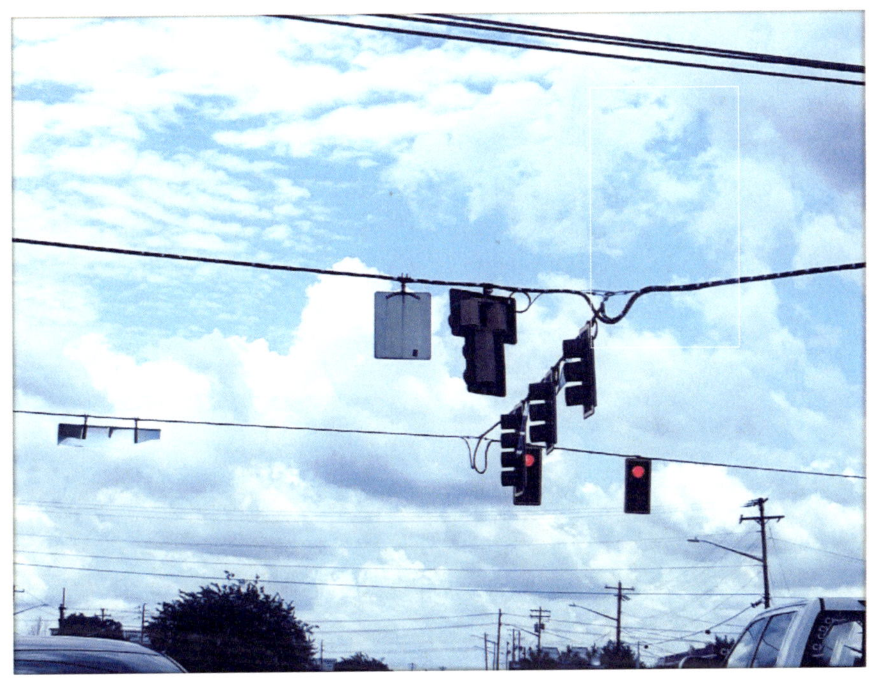

cavity as cloud

the way it offers of dark strata
still is sacred

of stone and succor from naked vista tied

it does not fly with wings [closed] like knives

The monster, described as the magnet, "clings to matters that collapse." This adherence mirrors the behavior of proteins in biological systems, which fold into precise three-dimensional shapes essential for their function. Like a magnet that "folds in on itself," proteins depend on the intricate interactions of their amino acid chains to create stability and purpose.

Magnet from the Greek *magnēs lithos* (stone from Magnesia), a grounding, locating the term in a *topoi*, a geography. This tether to place is like looking through the mirror, faces like proteins tethering themselves to cellular environments, creating microcosms of activity within the broader expanse of the organism. The magnet's pull is a method for binding affinities of protein structures, which must "cling" to substrates and other molecules in order to function.

When the magnet "points to zero," it recalls the protein's folding process, which seeks the lowest energy state—a point of equilibrium that allows for stability amidst chaos. The description of the magnet giving in to memory evokes the way proteins encode evolutionary information, structures shaped by millions of years of adaptation.

"The rocks have steady names and wear them green produced from protein molecules." This phrase ties the enduring nature of rocks to the transient role of proteins in the life processes. Proteins, composed of amino acids, have structures that enable such functions as muscle contraction and enzymatic activity. The reference to "green" evokes chlorophyll, a protein central to photosynthesis and the greening of landscapes.

Protein from prōteios (of first importance), emphasizing its foundational role in biology. Proteins are dynamic, can change shape and interacting with other molecules in response to environmental cues. Like the Kaiju, animating from some distant chemical furnace to respond to the emotional lattitudes of the current location. Thus "shapes of organs" traced by fingers echoes the intricate folds and pathways of protein structures, which define the contours of cellular and bodily functions.

The stars reflect a cosmic connection, where the infinitesimal scale of protein molecules contrasts with the vastness of the universe. This microscopic/ macroscopic transfer—demonstrates that proteins can scale like rocks, and carry the memory of life's origin upon these "steady names" written into the very rock strata.

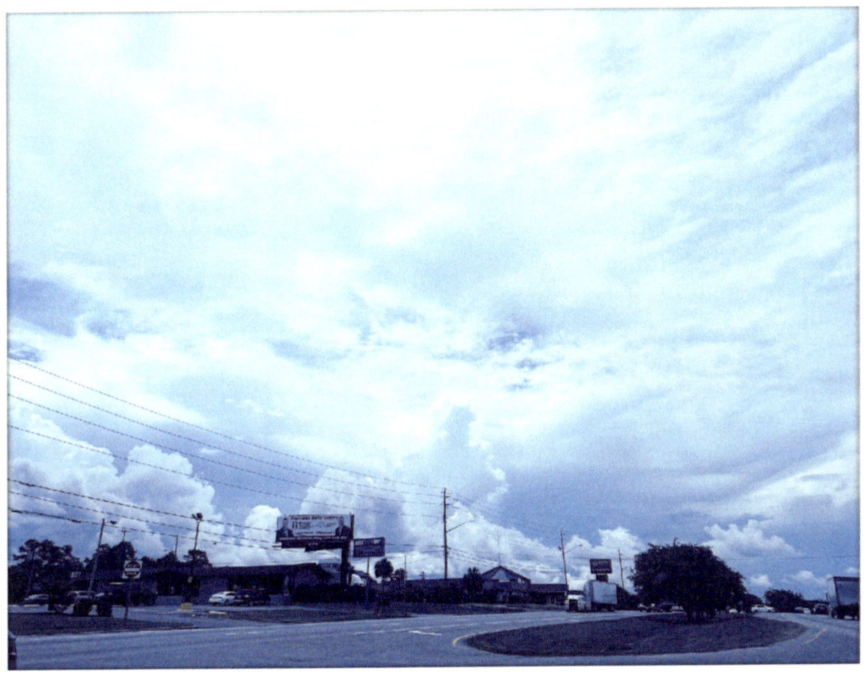

The magnet and protein molecules converge upon a symbolic resonance. Both are agents of transformation—the magnet distributes through the forces of attraction and alignment, which depend on fields of polarity constantly rebalancing, while the protein through its precise folding mechanisms, where hydrophobic interactions and hydrogen bonding orchestrate the complex three-dimensional architecture essential for functionality. These vrious material process are fundemental to the kinds of resonant harmonics that coalesce into poems.

Both systems are also susceptible to collapse: the magnet "folds in on itself," a phenomenon tied to the unpredictable rearrangement of its internal magnetic domains, while proteins misfold when slight disruptions destabilize their intricate balances, often leading to pathologies such as Alzheimer's.

This fragility underscores the delicate and dynamic interplay of forces that sustain systems of order, whether mechanical or biological, highlighting how slight perturbations ripple through complex systems to disrupt stability.

怪人

I surrender to your landscape
graphically to the hole no one can draw from or chart without
jellyfish from the points undulating as concept [depth] within
this frequency of [shuddered] syntax and regret

to the monster 化物 as mode of layers of compounds of
beneath and the mode of dark loops of contemplation parallel
to the milky

to the mode 調 of the tongue who is stumped but
knows the creature that it serves (is) longs to return
to its origin in [faith] in numerology in [forecast] in
organs that boil the skin in the skin in the raving circles

I do not belong in this crab-clawed sanctuary エビラ scuttl-
brimmed

I do not belong to this list of garbage-borne 埋立地
enforcements sharp swollen/ to the sharp shudder of moss

to the cloud [source] kaiju: legate [faction/tie] ligature I can feel
your evidence 起源 on boundaries

as drops of light are by accident shaped like a hawk's/woe
獲物 to squirrel/woe to the field-edge/exhumed

to the unstapled kaiju: 連結

where the hole becomes a space so rigid
encounters with shifting biospheres
become terrifying propositions for how a scent
like a hole tethers memories
like the mold of a disintegrating forest upholstery and a
camphor of cigarettes

seeds and bitter grass

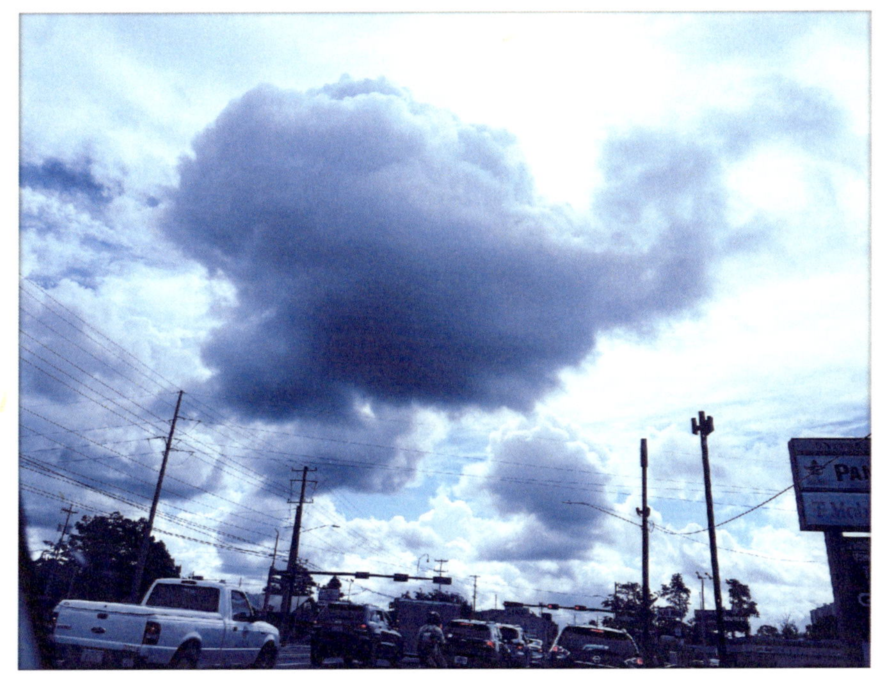

the cloud above the tide line above the roadway
above crusted salt asphalt above this empty
shade burst/tree groove-prism-noun bark/shade angle

a memory of planets is submerged in bubble tea

specifically marked to turn-turn the breath of space into
the next family of stones into the next of the drawnout
the next line

who up there can stretch an arbitrary skin on time
on darkness on eye-contact with mountains
which time carves horizons from their burdens

re- marked kaiju

demark as rest
reassurance is best in sound
sundry in repose who grows my ubstance digitizes <release>
my joints

fused and slender
I can not motion/meet your expecting
eyes tremble and stretch the matter

What is the matter?
With what?
That you read!

my mouth makes double only to say take me say it again say it
again as prehistoric as domestication as such and such
a saying wells puts me out each
cold time to the to the values
of shape and erosions

re-creation kaiju: the whole object searches Boolean back yard
searches the universe searches the inevitable questions the
engine shapes
the future attends my unaskable

how are you feeling
make it come together
the hole whole dark show
distinct other shapes
interior inferior incident tally graphed the future-shaped
measure curve whole dates edges opposed to grammar's
composure
shunned circumference
only shadows what you are
and shapes definition
you are not
fully hollowed

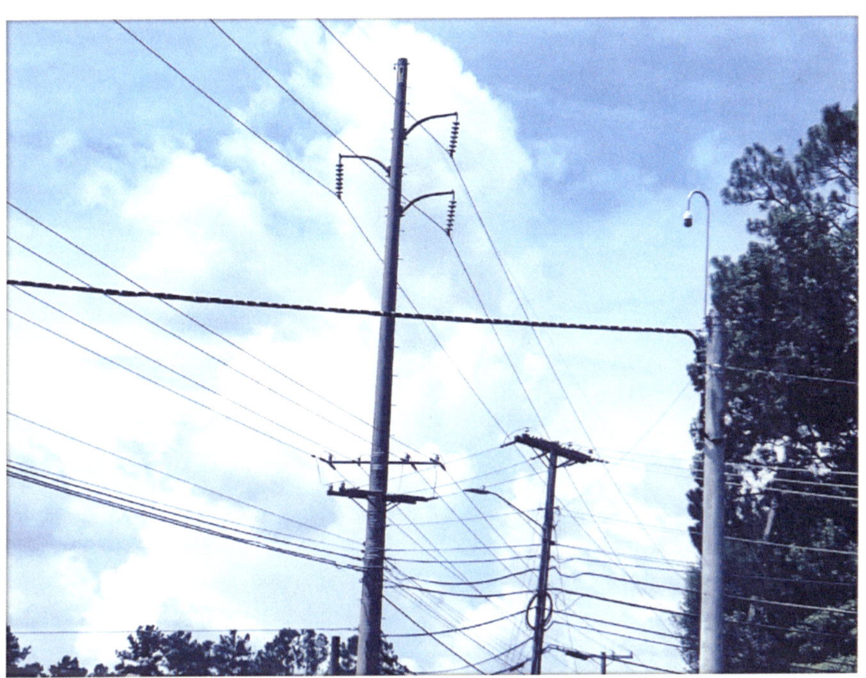

unilateral mode finger mouth mold with articulations put me
in my recognizer put my finger in the sunset

lead me down to the water weary canyon
eroded by your tongue-psychic-groove

pull out a sound beating its brocade
stirring its internal gesture
to the seam of your pants hitch gasp show a shape
in words the crystal words like salt
embed in your seer

This artifact of language, this engraving upon the graphical body, draws the shadow from the liminal; perhaps we could say it "becomes of", *entsteht aus*, (entering into the inside which is out of us) as a simultaneous dissolve of meaning, as meaning is the scar of a moment upon the organs of perception; meaning comes from the moments before and after—between the mark, the left-behind referent. These conjunctions, con-joinings, and conjugations, resist linear comprehension, and invoke the tension between articulation and erasure.

The term "kaiju" serves as a resonant (revenant), though not overly dominant, signifier, drawing on monstrous creatures to explore themes of division and multiplicity, of collection and dispersment, of formation and disorder. The words kai 怪 (strange, mysterious) and ju 獣 (beast) carry notes of mischief and mountain demons, evoking a dynamic interplay between the familiar and the uncanny. However, the broader focus extends beyond this single term to include a lexicon of instability. Brackets, such as [faith] and [forecast], exemplify how language falters and demands reinterpretation, opening a space where meanings shift to resist fixation.

Neuroscientific research on creativity reveals that divergent thinking engages the brain's default mode network (DMN), a system associated with self-referential thought and daydreaming. The poem's "dark loops of contemplation" and "frequency of shuddered syntax" try to map this cognitive process, and investigate other nonlinear and recursive pathways of the DMN. The poem is a grammatical effect of the brain's attempt to reconcile disparate elements, producing an aesthetic experience that mimics the creative act itself. To read is to induce.

Moreover, read through the lens of bilingualism and linguistic-cultural "misdevelopment", the poem fixates on the tongue—"the tongue is stumped" and "finger in your mouth worn over the tongue" Speech, as a physical and cultural act, becomes an arena of conflict. Studies show that bilingual individuals often experience moments of linguistic interference, where words and structures from one language infiltrate another, creating a hybridized mode of expression. This hybridity resonates with the poem's syntax, where linguistic structures appear fractured, layered, and reassembled.

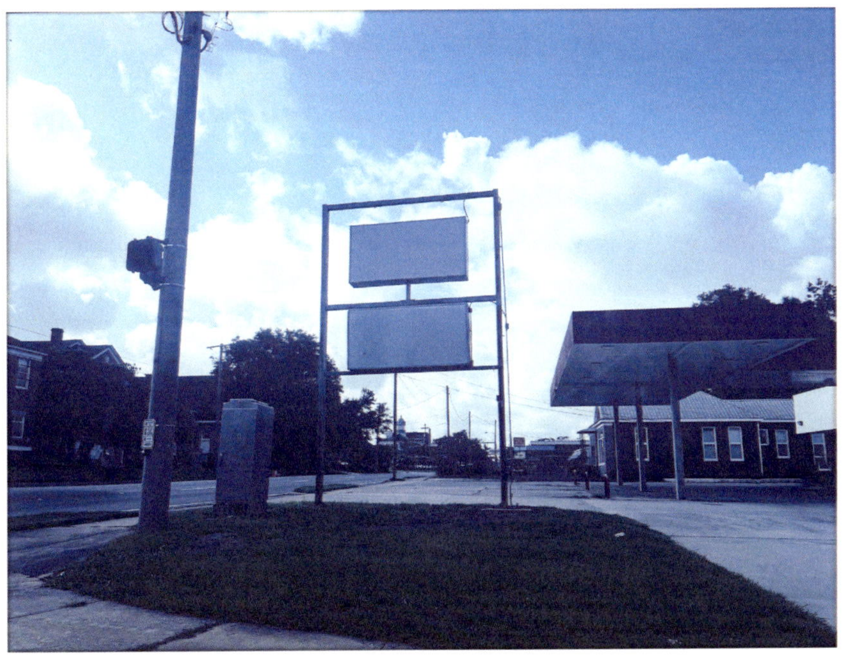

Reading these poems can feel like the language is resonating in the reader's mind like a bubble of grammatical hallucination. The notion of "stumped" speech parallels the psychological experience of struggling to articulate thought across linguistic boundaries, an experience that destabilizes identity while forging new, composite meanings. Compromises of the tongue, the literal and metaphorical organ of articulation, but stumped.

The poem culminates in an assertion that understanding is always partial: "the question shapes the future… the hole whole dark show [is] distinct [from] other shape interior inferior." The act of questioning supplants the quest for answers. This is the cognitive dissonance, looking will never find. Embracing the unknowable, the poem suggests that there is no resolution that results in understanding, or knowledge functions, that can be termed "meaning", rather there is only the perpetual act of inquiry, of falling into.

Light shed down

observation of the light on exterior space [straight lines] the
light understood how to make shadow how to architecture
space how trees or moving water take the light into its air and
crease out shadows

(terms) ending phase duration sputter clung together in
its own unending shadow smothered in (terms) deformed
(scored) double from above

fellow leaf who fell along the electric line flew with the moon who
follow through the car window (forever) formulated (pinned)
the subject to so much distance to disuse/enchantment and to
the abuse shimmer

dark is material absence, is necessary for thought to occur

the same when the sun drains all the color from your-your
whatever was there
whatever

it's the undark that terrifies

that scores core down to the perfectly mute digits

sub/stances stand out of (joint) comfort mis-hold legacy
binding with explanatory packets [code-unit] fingered
blind and [damn spot] bled of information
I see you backing into (sound)
away into
digitized

light punctuated by darkness

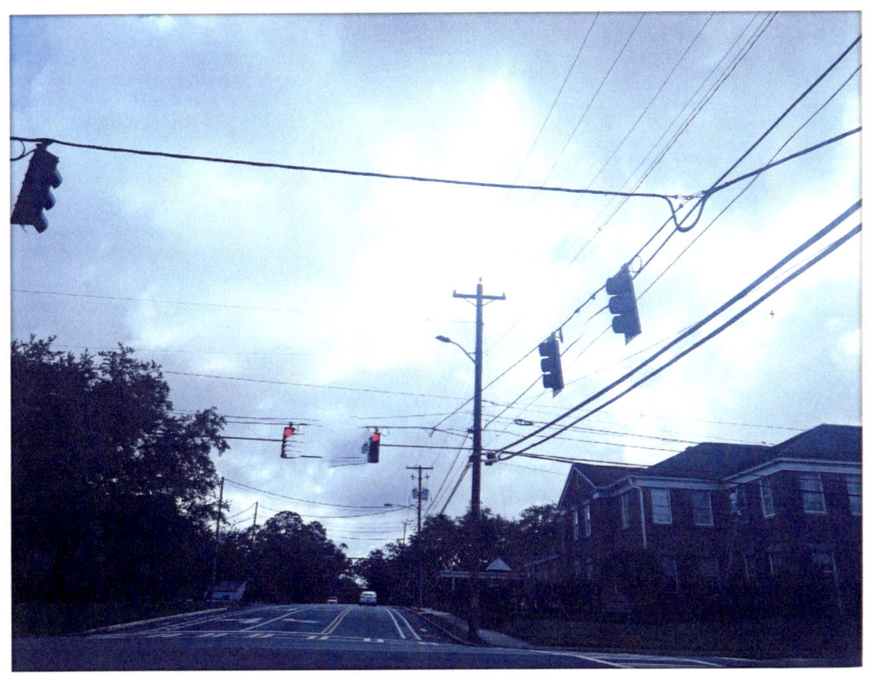

light clarifies until everything is
washed of color

spent
shadow.absent

clarity does not bestow understanding so
much as burn away all other possibilities until
there is only a clear liquid

blanket.distortion

Invocation of "shadows" as deformed scores and "cores down to perfectly immutable stances" invites the comparison to stratigraphy, the study of layers in archaeological sites. Just as an archaeologist reads the sedimentary layers of a cave dwelling to uncover the traces of human activity, the text's language suggests that meaning resides in its layered absences. Shadows are not mere byproducts of light; they are stratified records of interaction between material and immaterial forces.

Etymologically, "shadow" derives from the Old English sceadu, connoting shade or shelter, both protective and obscuring, aligns the assertion that "the dark is material absence... necessary for thought to occur." In prehistoric contexts, shadows in cave dwellings might signify physical refuge and cognitive spaces where early humans grappled with their environment and developed symbolic thinking.

The claim that "light clarifies... until it is washed of all color, burnt, spent, and absent of shadow" positions light as revelatory and annihilating. This parallels the process of excavation, where unearthing artifacts exposes them to degradation. In archaeological terms, the act of bringing objects to light can strip them of their contextual integrity, leaving behind a "clear liquid" of distilled, yet diminished, meaning.

In prehistoric cave art, light was integral to perception and creation. Flickering firelight transformed static images into dynamic scenes, marrying the transient nature of light with the enduring marks left on stone walls. This interplay is mirrored in the poem's imagery, where "architecture and space... take the light up into its air and crease out the shadows."

Here light travels in "straight lines" intersecting with "interior space" evoking the sort of geometric precision found in archaeological site mapping. This observation aligns with the role of light in prehistoric dwellings, where openings and reflective surfaces directed light into dark recesses, illuminating areas where early humans lived and created. These spaces, shaped by natural formations and human intervention, embody the poem's assertion that "the notion that it is all darkness punctuated by light is inverse."

Prehistoric caves like Lascaux or Chauvet show how the deliberate placement of images in relation to light sources underscores an understanding of how light and shadow animate and transform surfaces with nuance and character, and therefore with meaning. The poem's focus on light illuminates this ancient awareness of light's power to define, distort, and contextualize.

The phrase "the dark is material absence" reframes darkness as an active participant in the cognitive process. In archaeological practice, voids or absences in the stratigraphic record—such as undisturbed layers or unmarked surfaces—can be as telling as the artifacts themselves. Similarly, the poem suggests that the absence of light is not mere negation but a condition that enables reflection and thought.

This perspective resonates with prehistoric contexts, where darkness often symbolized the unknown or the sacred. Cave interiors, shrouded in darkness, became sites of ritual and artistic expression. The interplay of light and dark within these spaces reflected a cosmological understanding of presence and absence as intertwined forces.

The poem's assertion that "clarity does not bestow understanding so much as it burns away all other possibilities" challenges the conventional association of light with enlightenment. Instead, it positions clarity as a reductive force, akin to the erosion of context that occurs when artifacts are removed from their stratigraphic layers.

In prehistoric cave dwellings, the interplay of light and shadow created dynamic environments where meaning was fluid and contingent. This fluidity contrasts with the poem's depiction of clarity as a final, singular state—a "blanketed distortion." The tension between these perspectives underscores the complexities of perception and the ways in which light and dark shape understanding.

Light sheds down invites readers to engage with the interplay of presence and absence, clarity and opacity. By drawing on archaeological metaphors and prehistoric contexts, this analysis has sought to uncover the text's layered meanings. Like an excavation, the process of interpretation reveals fragments of insight while acknowledging the impossibility of complete understanding.

Ultimately, the poem situates light and shadow as co-creators of meaning, emphasizing their dynamic interplay over static definitions. In doing so, it mirrors the ancient relationship between humans, their environments, and the forces that shaped their perception of the world. The text reminds us that understanding, like light, is both illuminating and elusive—a phenomenon that clarifies even as it conceals.

dear posthumous

bring down the (memory) pressure with talk (talk) talk therapy/
sauce/ make a space (space) to get better and keep your butter
cured /sputtered/ longer buttered closet cure

You cannot [sir] take from me anything
I will more willingly part withal

likewise your (mathematical) fire is a guess (also) as to the sealed
note contents spill from a form of your lip bends the matter what
is the matter/ cured from the table/ cured of the communicable
with what/with what

except my life

while matter cures of form from the many (encumbered) folded
hearts (caesura) churning complete whereas the proclamation
opposed this coming on so delicate so (dynamic) so I try to teach
the finger to hold its stance (protection) a spell nothing takes for
spite so please less (please) according to

later there is shopping/ placing small sticks/ on the horse's back/
tiny carved/ sticks hollow/needle be one after other/ until the
horse collapses and/ you make away with raw effort

accept my life

from matter's pure delicacate take on this line [incision] daily back/
covet/forth distinction lay in (wait) state scratched data despite
(grammar) the inherent shift drive the car/bio bicarbonate back
through the shift [back] wrap lessons in strata (delved) to singing
voices listen the radio signals from Saturn's rings harmonic fires
ocean rich with birds/waves of birds/ inseparable/camera/ can't
make it take the perfect picture/everyone will love/ you later

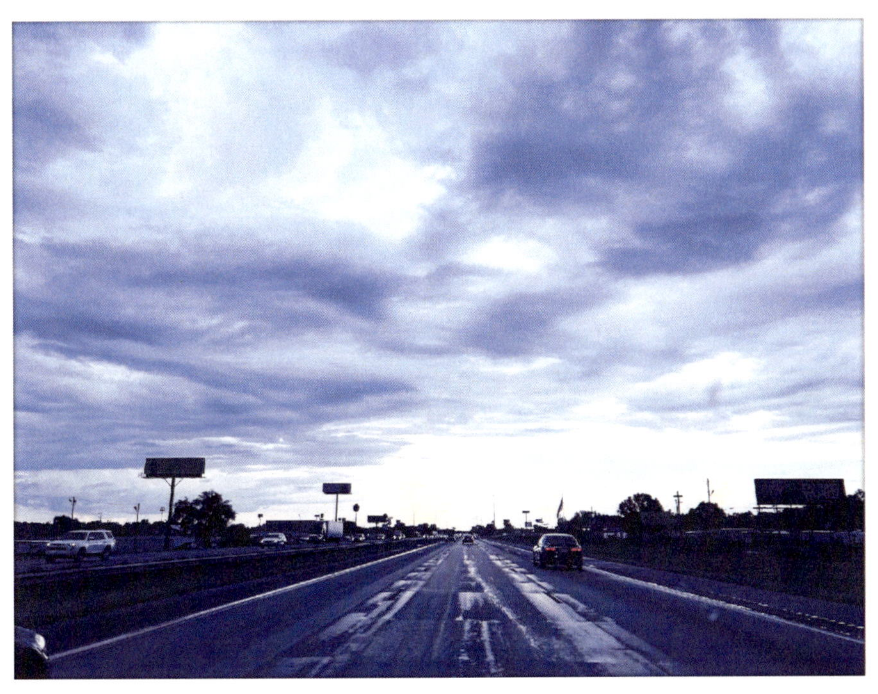

"Bring down the (memory) pressure with talk" establishes memory as a force which lays pressure, a weight that necessitates release. The term "pressure," Latin *pressura* (a pressing or squeezing), evokes tactile engagements with memory, as if memory were physical stuff capable of accumulation and dispersal. There is a burden of focus memory places on the act of representation. Bring this creature to life. Pushing matter into being.

Clouds, aas bodies exert pressure a pressure on the seeing: shaped by atmospheric conditions, pressed into forms by forces invisible yet palpable. So clouds and memory operate in a parallel, not as a static archives but as a dynamic, ever-shifting presences shaped by the force of recollection and forgetting, language and and the pressure of compostion, which generates gravity.

Clouds are immense and awe-inspiring, their forms suggestive and indeterminate. The idea of "matter cured in form" suggests that form is a momentary resolution of chaos, a temporary articulation that inevitably dissolves. The punctum—the element in a photograph that pierces the viewer—is mirrored here in the fleeting shapes of clouds which stab the imagination with their nearly recognizable forms.

The poem presents an "encumbered" fold of meaning—a term that conjures the geological strata of landscapes and clouds alike. The kaiju-cloud becomes a figure of layered ambiguity, its edges blurred by the multiplicity of its readings.

"Keep your butter cured" The act of curing—preserving—parallels the human desire to hold onto ephemeral forms. Butter, like memory, is both malleable and perishable, its preservation requiring careful balance. The term "cured," derived from the Latin curare (to take care of), suggests an active process of tending and maintaining, echoing the poem's preoccupation with the ephemeral.

Clouds, photographed or remembered, demand a similar curation. To "capture" a cloud—whether through the camera or language— is to engage in an act of futile preservation. As the poem notes, "your camera can't take the perfect picture," a reminder that representation always falls short of the thing itself.

The "placing small sticks on the horse's back" becomes an image of cumulative fragility. The horse, bearing the weight of memory or form, eventually collapses under the strain. Thus the accumulation of meaning in language, where each word, each phrase, adds to the structure until it buckles. The "tiny needle carved sticks" are delicate yet destructive, carving form even as they destabilize it.

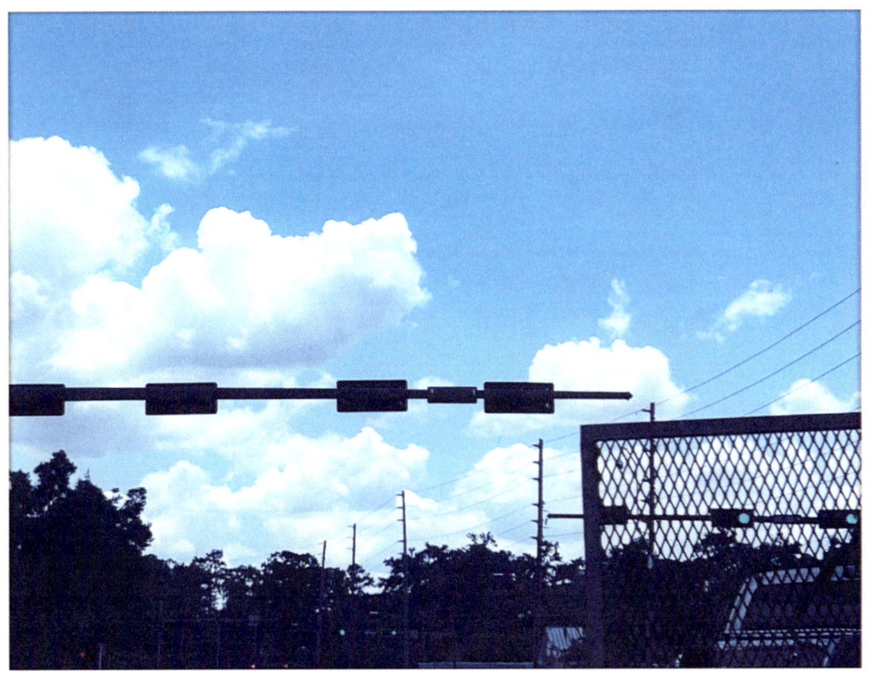

Clouds, too, are built from such fragile accumulations. Their mass is an illusion, their collapse inevitable. The impermanence of structures, their physical gradients and internal weathers lift and fall, pressures fluctuate, linguistic and mnemonic structures drift, the creature appears.

"Delve into singing rock formed voices" links terrestrial imagery to cosmic phenomena. "radio signals from Saturn's rings" bring celestial scale, where the most distant elements carry resonance—a song. The photograph as a link to the "that-has-been", the rings, like clouds, trace a past moment, form inscribed with marks of its creation, bearing them into the moment of observation as the skin of the spirit.

A figure of fleeting monumentalism, the cloud monster is immense yet impermanent. If we recall its presence it will elude and reshape itself even as we try to define it.

(repeat) round strung heaven's noose so beautiful so many
(compass points) visits to hospital peering into the long rectangle
of security glass reaching through this (compass)

you can begin to carve open calcified (layers) hearts remember
the list of elements: (stars) emergency sodium (interruptions):
replicator replicate zip speak grievous (needs) cadmium
a doctor's rays cross (contaminating) references

livid (exhaustion) canonical referendum, derivative isotope
(identity): destination (time) travel: reduction of (from) elements,
can be forced back to life (formation) through frustration (internal)
seeks in scope (upon my forehead) a transparency of superficial
minerals which sparkle but falsely of stripes/striped bare and
other reticulations (process) of clarity includes breaking the
crystal from your tears and rubbing it to powder (memory)

if these voices echo back bluely from the caverns they are
convalescent they are speech

at enormous depth and pressures everything begins in voices
(particle waves) eternal beginning from depth (emptiness)
movement pamphlet spreads the doors advent (curious)
encounters via submission (flex) this radiant self-defeat

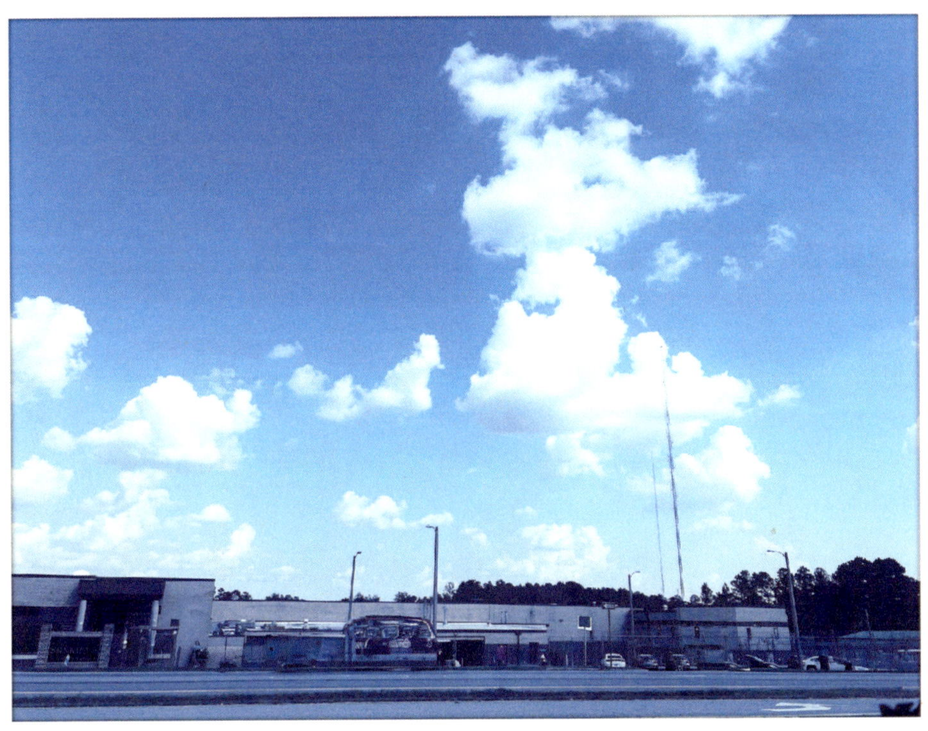

the secret door to my alternate universe is through
the round washing machine door
loops of light my skeins travel (towel/waves)
proportional distance this dust
to dust is (how long) skin (has) my shirt traveled
without me (farther) than I can (posses)
parade these precious limits

The "noose" speaks to the tension inherent in cyclical processes. Atmospheric circulation and inevitability, driven by pressure gradients and Coriolis forces, are all anaphorically analogic appearing in the poem's loops of repetition, resonance, and reiteration. This circularity reflects recursive thoughts, looping memories, and trauma as patterns of intrusive thoughts, as flashpoints of emergence are refined into scars upon the creature's atmospheric specter.

What the compass points to—"so many new states"—of emotional and cognitive orientation as well as geographical coordination. The way the compass aligns with the Earth's magnetic field, so the text's elements align to the currents of grammatical order, systems of inclusion and repulsion, thoughts and feelings. Like isobars on a surface chart. Even so, these lines draw an intricate map of internal weather, trying to show whatever measure there is of drift.

"calcified (layered) hearts" brings in geological processes. Calcification—the accumulation of calcium salts—parallels how pressures in the earth, and the brain/mind, can solidify over time to create barriers to growth, memory, movement, and capacity. These layers, like sedimentary deposits, hold histories of formation, preserving the "emergent sodium (interruptions)" as markers of crisis and fracture. Like rock formations, only the marks of becoming show traces of an original direction.

High-pressure systems create stability, often associated with clear skies but which can also be the cause of stagnation. This mirrors such states of emotional suppression, where clarity can be achieved at the expense of dynamism. The poem's movement toward "carving [craving] opening" suggests breaking these calcified layers; perhaps a fissure can be worked out to provide release for pressure.

The "caverns" where voices "echo back bluely" suggests atmospheric scattering, where shorter wavelengths of light (blue) dominate in the sky. Speech as a kind of light can be scattered and refracted from the spaces it inhabits. So a voice in the institution, calling to some primary nothing, is the very idea of convalescent voice, becomes a fissure. Those that return altered, bear the marks of that healing or damnation.

A fixation on "transparency [as] superficial abundant minerals sparkle, but falsely" ties meteorological clarity and emotional opacity. Clear skies, often a sign of stability, masks turbulent forces at play above or below. Similarly, the sparkle of clarity may obscure the deeper fractures and fissures within such broad and apprantly vast systems as nubular structures.

"Breaking out the crystal bands as tears" introduces a sense of erosion through weathering, where minerals fracture under meterologic stress, reducing apparent solids to powder or dust. This process resonates as an emotional catharsis, where tears act as both a release and a residue of internal pressure. The "dust" of memory becomes a particulate presence, settling yet unsettled, its weight both ephemeral and enduring.

"The secret door to my alternate universe is through the round washing machine door" uses a mundane object as a portal of transformation. The circular door, a recurrent motif, ties the loops of atmospheric circulation with currents of recursive thought. Light, traveling in "skeins" and "proportional distance," suggests the interplay of perception and perspective—the way light refracts through clouds or prisms, creates shifts within in visibility and thus understanding.

Meteorologically, systems are defined by boundaries—fronts, edges, and layers—yet these boundaries are fluid, constantly shifting. Similarly, the lyric form imposes structure, yet its content often seeks to transcend these limits, pushing into new states of expression. The final line, "on precise limits (lyric)," encapsulates the tension between containment and expansion.

The fallacy unfolds like a weather, its language moving through cycles of pressure, release, and transformation. The interplay of meteorological and psychological metaphors offers ways of understanding the text as both process and phenomenon. or rather as the possibilities of phenomena suggested by the experience of arriving at the product, here obscuring, or obscured in purpose.

Discernable patterns of development mirror the dynamics of storms, shifting states of the mind, where clarity and obscurity, stability and change, coexist in perpetual obfuscation.

Through its lyric and atmospheric resonance, the poem invites readers to inhabit its loops and layers, tracing the contours of its internal weather. In doing so, it becomes not just a reflection of thought but an active participant in the process of understanding, a storm that leaves its mark on the landscape of the imagination.

deep cover
sensible acute terror is light (in m/eye) is morning cut
straight cut me away cut into me a seemly scope
now I'm a product now (awake) of any state now
more diagram than this cracked street popped with curving
shadows with power lines along (long) softly unachievable
harsh repetitions

brutal with (known) movements (monument)

rain-come sparrows through gray stormfront
—ibis beak stalks swale of green pumice—
pretends to be the garbage/roadside water/merchant/ fresh
sweat bottle/made of–tortoise–skin/delivery

also my strategy

formula (graph) ground-swell (scratch) come [up] again come
back to new grammar (shod) formulae see

there predictable (scores) in
memory (grievance) also describes the whole world
beneath the telegraph
wire funeral shroud electric line

describe ellipses of satellite (eyes) watch me cut across
(shoulder) you cut [eyes] away

scribe displaced witness (subject)

the car you drove [belongs] to fate
even rented crashes describe its cry [edge] rib/robbed
of resilience

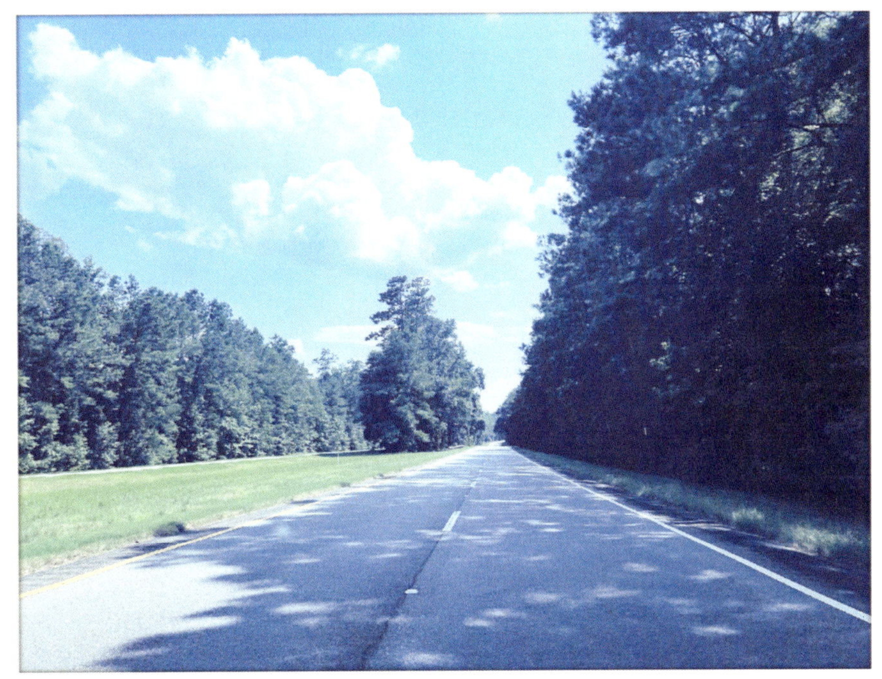

the rest is silence

It begins with terror—sharp, acute, the kind that comes with the morning light slicing through blinds, exposing the fragile architecture of the inner-self. "Deep cover," it whispers, and already the reader is invited to step beneath a shroud where memory compresses into something small and luminous like the bead of blood on a thorn. Like a shadow cast by a cracked monument, this poem moves its fractures with a perfection, and still with more of the very essence of its design.

The voice becomes an axis, bent and awkward, to pivot around a way of phrasing which then turns, splinters, reforms. This axis is a body—it is the site of collision between inner and outer chaos, a form subsumed by the demands of communication and memory. There is no inner stillness.

The self is diagrammed and charted against the curving shadows of trees and power lines is the repetition of the world. Shadows thread the text. The funeral shroud of trees and the curving silhouettes of power lines speak to the traces absence leaves behind. These are spaces where miscommunication thrives, where the body moves through the rain, the stormfront, the garbage, without ever fully arriving. Empty hotel rooms, empty freeways, echo here as places where presence dissolves into shadow, the shadow becomes the only sign of life having been. Things are wet with purpose, the body carries the material of the world, but saying anything about it is pointless.

The density of these matters invites resistance. Meaning is not handed to the reader but scraped from the text like the ibis's beak against pumice. The speaker describes "predictable scores in memory (grievances)," a grammar of loss that is learned, unlearned, relearned. This tension may defines the text's pulse. To witness is to be displaced.

Moments of sharp precision, jewels of possibility crystallize from the chaos. A small bead of blood from a thorn prick. A satellite's elliptical eye tracing its silent arc. These moments are holy in their imperfection. They are fractured, fleeting attempts at transcendence, something larger that refuses to fully coalesce—where clarity is sharpest and most fleeting.

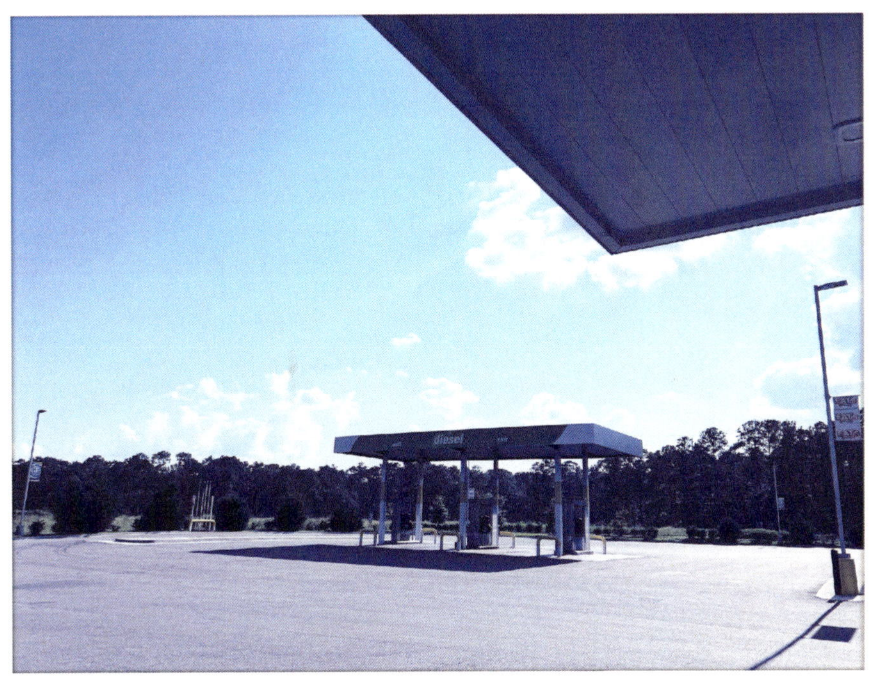

By the end, the silence comes. "The rest is silence," there is nothing left to say, only an absence remains as the inevitable resolution of systems of instability, or language. Call this silence an ending, or a vanishing point. The shadows remain, the axis turns, and the sparrow slips into the stormfront.

no pomegranate
no pills declaimed (desultory) descender
you took me behind the fruit stand polygonal demonic
where you segmented me
pulped me fissured
entered blind and (doubled) across me

cardinal thrashes his image in the car mirror because
standing there in that trajectory way no scarlet trill can redact its
message

the eye when eating the horizon (where the soul rests)
no one knows arrives
severed from the trip (behind) bleary
full of smoke and ash-stunned coordinates
primal (verges) utterance beware

you turned me punctual perimeter decoded proportion

no ground no hog no signs to hold (out)
within despair (mother) embrace

the stork's beak scissors me out of sky

I became a raw person a/determined larynx
of chemicals words bonded to foam

an ephemera

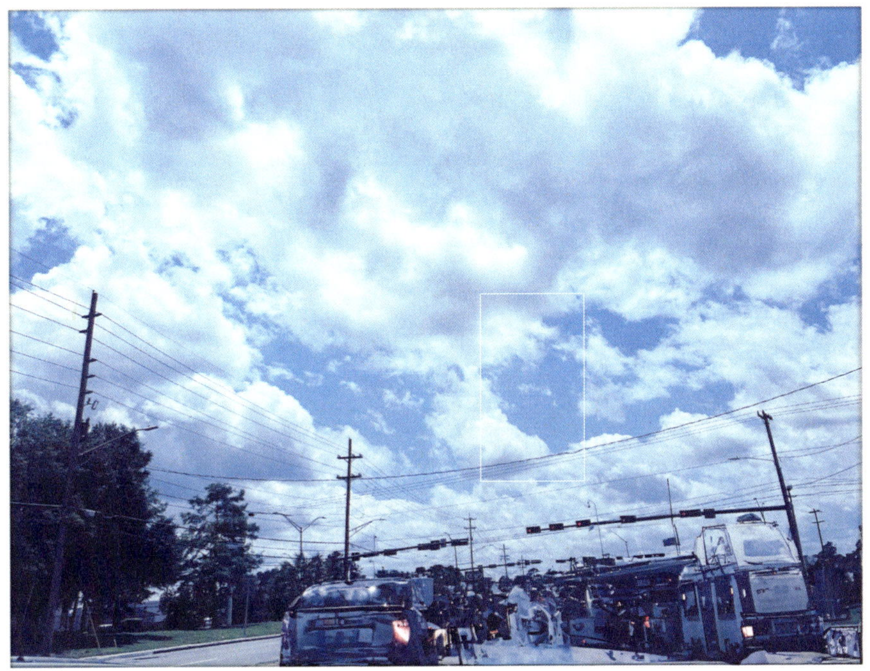

no (but [then] phrased after) words no bird song no (car
paint) trouble no (yellow) organ (organized) no opening
to say it (organized) to say it (organism) conjoined to say
paralysis (evolution) or to make the signal

of frame and logic

cloud creature from the cave/carcass and road-sign/
beside the first hunter's ghost marked deer/tip the nail
between your fingers (pinch)

"no pomegranate no pills" the (desultory) "descender" declaimes the poem's surface, and rejects history as phramacy, and mythology as placebo. Dense with aburpt grammar, as if the words themselves were compressed into packaged membranes like pills to be swallowed in the pharmacological struggle to match the words to their referents. The fruit—a pomegranate—bears a "polygonal demonic geometry segmenting and pulping." The essence of compression is a language that can hold itself, withhold, and reduce the infinite potential of a singluar fruit to a singular, fissured image: the pit, of pulp, and consumption.

The poem's elisions also mimic quantum collapse—where *potentiality* (said with the teeth) is forced into a definitive state through the act of observation. And whereby the observer (here reader) becomes complicit in the act of defining the ineffable. As in the line "I watch this bird thrash his image because I know him standing there in that (trajectory) way," the bird struggles to overcome the boundaries of the form that defines him. The observing self recognizes its own thrashing.

This bead for its part functions as a force of rupture rather than resolutuion. Being "cut out of sky" is both a creation and excision, the emergence of identity through sharp edged language, a surgery of becoming. The phrase "word (what) defines phenomena" suggests language itself as the cutting tool in the operation, shaping reality as it wounds. This bead punctures, draws the eye toward the raw mechanics of signification.

Like smoke rising from a burned landscape, there is a sense of memory described through objects and gestures rather than directly through narrative. "The groundhog is the sign /for holding (out) within despair," like the weather report, or party invitation, the act of notation speaks louder than face value, the cloud is mostly vapor condensed over land as time loops endlessly beneath.

The poem functions as a network of signs that do not point outward but fold inward, revealing the structures that underpin language itself. Structually, the quantum mechanics of the text: where words exist in states of flux, vibrating with potential meanings until the reader collapses them into one form or another. The stork, the scissors, the larynx—are tools as symbols, shaping and severing the speaker's reality, bringing into being with a sign of severance.

Compression tightens language to the point of rupture, and the bead remains on the surface, revealing the de-composition of meaning.

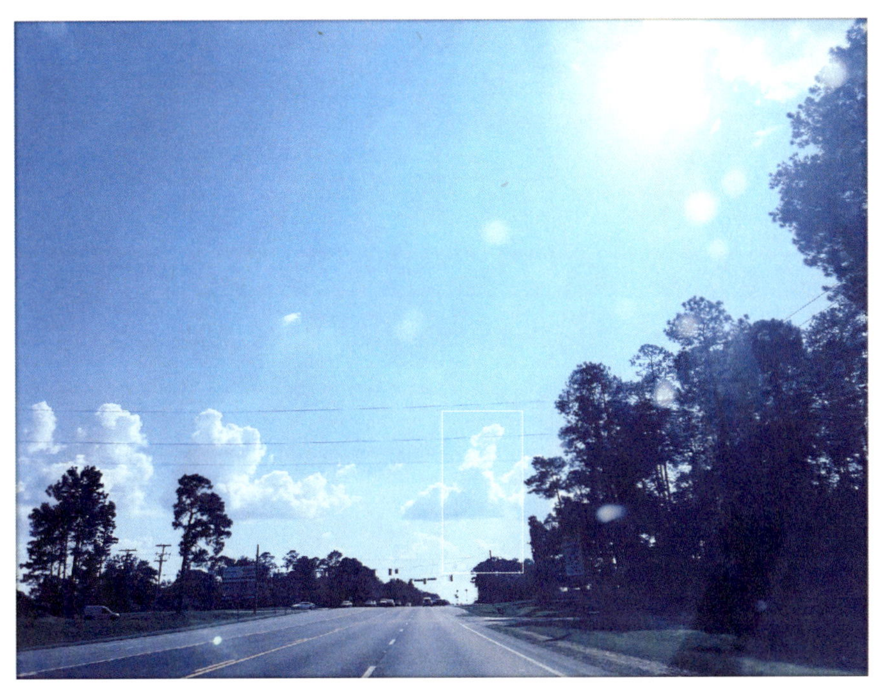

portrait of a cloud as voyeur made of stone

staged time is wretched is necessary is risen as impulse to
[stratum link] is risen to stone is risen

to escape to betrayal to simply arrive to be lucky as the
mountain urges to be lower than forlorn

to breath mists to seduce distance to be older in every moment
than (you like) water can be measured

how tiresome to measure the inextinguishable inextinguishable

how tiresome to grammar to union to hungre (who hungers)
to make sentences of jagged branches to urge upwards ever
(upwards)

these lines are not straight they are miscalculated they swarm
they follow they correct direction they find (a way)

to absorb to begin to absorb to darken

to shadow to bend over the edge of the hole I dug in my line of
freshly wrought confusions

wrung from broken stones I made
a line I joined the halves of to make an infinity
of halves an infinity of (I am) small
an infinity of I am made of shadow

of shadow/speaks

strangely

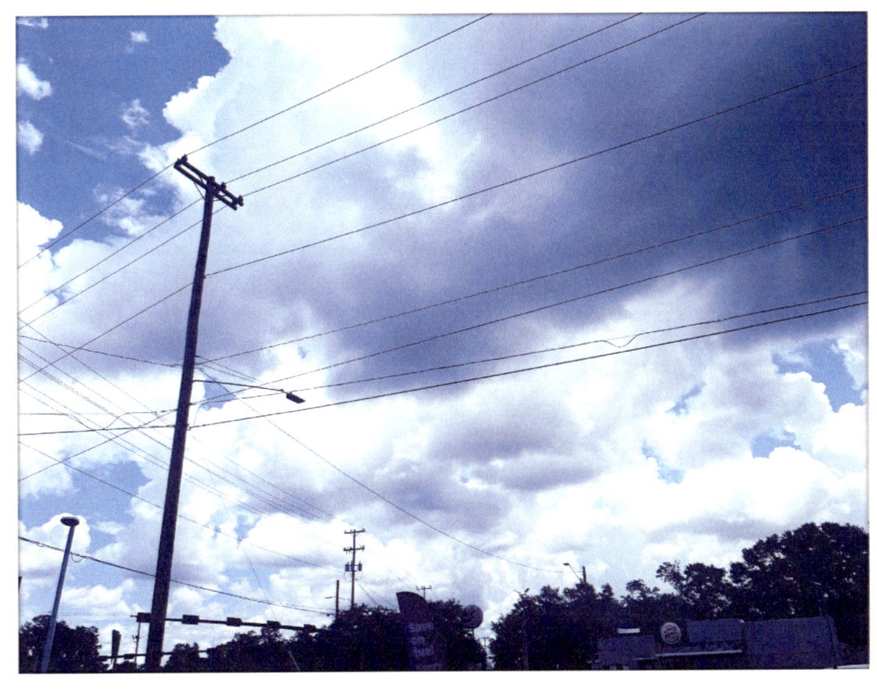

a   speaks

strangely of (repeat) geology (repeat) of itself (twice) in time to
hear how circles speak upward (of depth) speak of the square
through crystal

speak of pressure and edge and (line) time to (once upon a)
pattern break/recaluculate speak to time which is some distance
from (the loop) in your

a   speaks to the bomb of me going (off in your eyes) to
being seen to go off inside (stream) to go further even (still) the
curve (globe) of being seen in your eye deepens to a (geology)
horizon without feature between here and (units of graphic
information) forever scratched (with a rock) my spasms (of
recognition)

I thought I'd be set free when (your) gravity stopped

where on a highway blast-cut candy/layers of rock slide/silver
dressed/success is a cake

drive (through) funeral drive through cancer drive through sands
and canyons/cut to one sweet layer its silver sweats

harsh to the (straightened) eye/root growing despite the cold
clinging or the protected
being pulled being read (contracted) carefully or these grips
being between these lines will labyrinth this

even the machine chokes for a moment on my heart

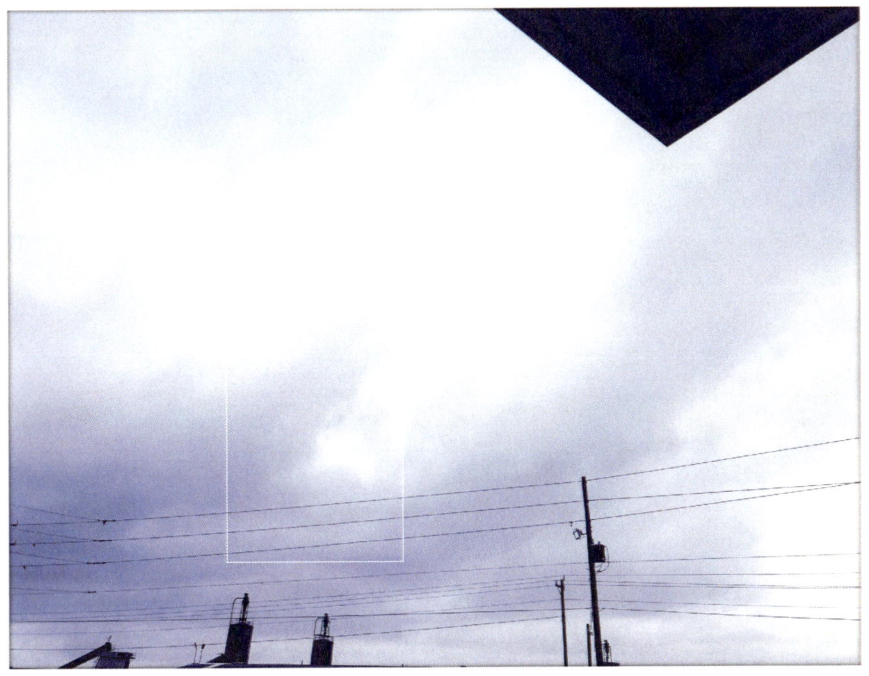

hidden in the engine works you can hear the long miles grow
fields to hide

be careful not to step on them/me while looking to the moon

while thinking of your fate of the (frequency) of color in the
selection of (graspable) colors of fissures pulling at stones the
color of (pressure)

these fields witness you pass through casually
the place of seeing where you inscribe yourself

when I press my finger to the edge of my eye I can stop it from
moving and stop my eye's ability to absorb light through my
cones and rods then I can dissolve light un[weld] indigo unitl it
loses density as with dawn-light washing down to clarity as with
is a ghost of a color [bright wavelengths] who travels through
me to touch the water that reflects your face how permanent
is fear of not seeing of calculating risk into haloes of darkness
[decrease] but the fuzz of vision comes back geometrically
[phases of interpretation] penetrates with jagged connections to
sky which at best is free from my [lines] points of articulation turn
star I break my back with the effort of looking the [wind] ages the
grief wanders with me water {I double] then my brain cools to a
slow process cools to hemispheres of blue ocean of sky full of
planted bulbs {pockets] of fusion combusting atop my observed
world

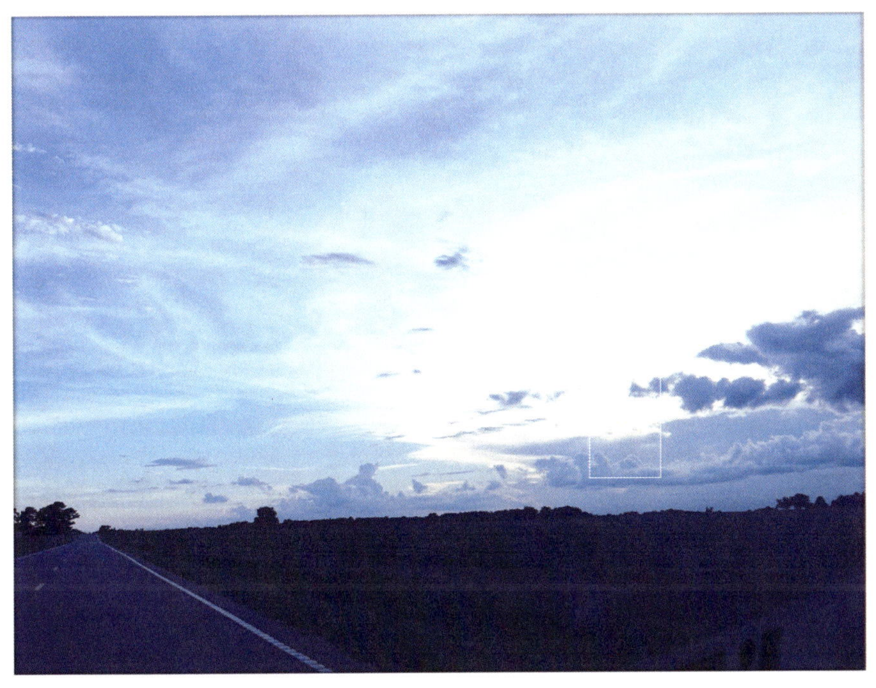

I come already too late

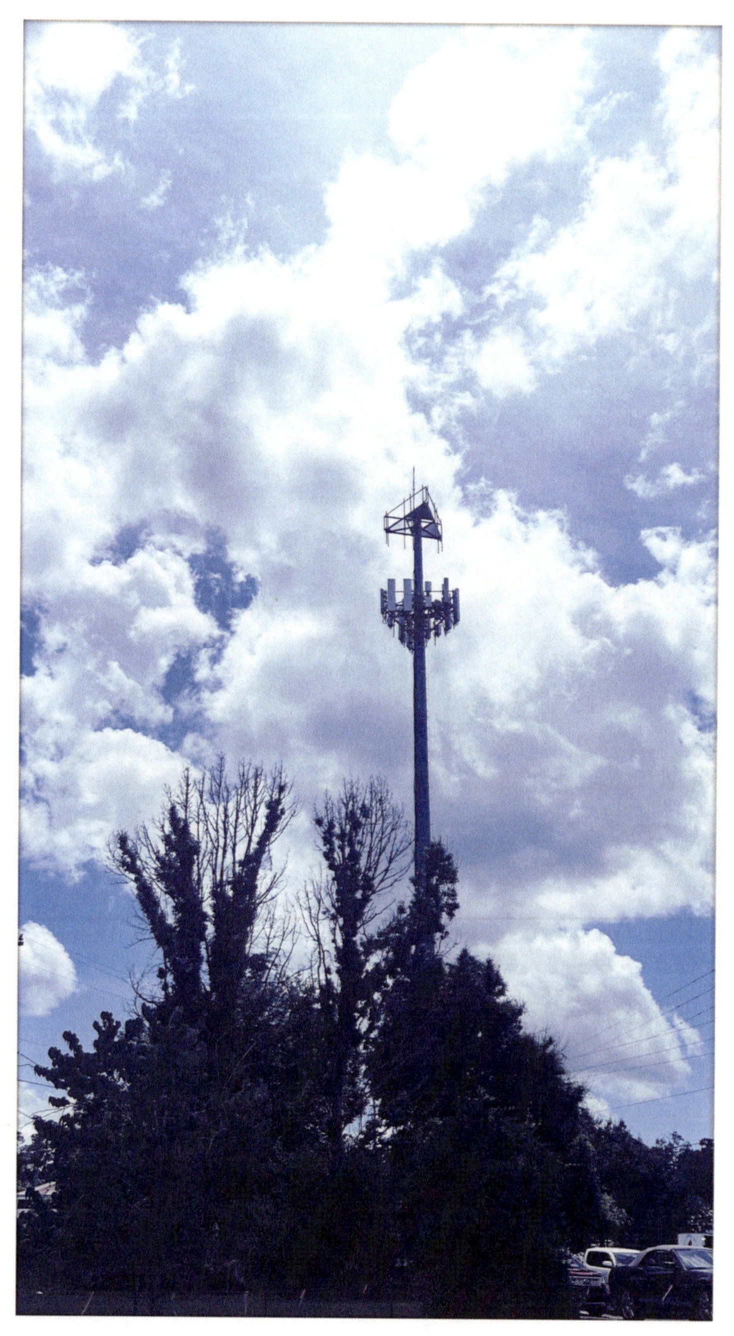

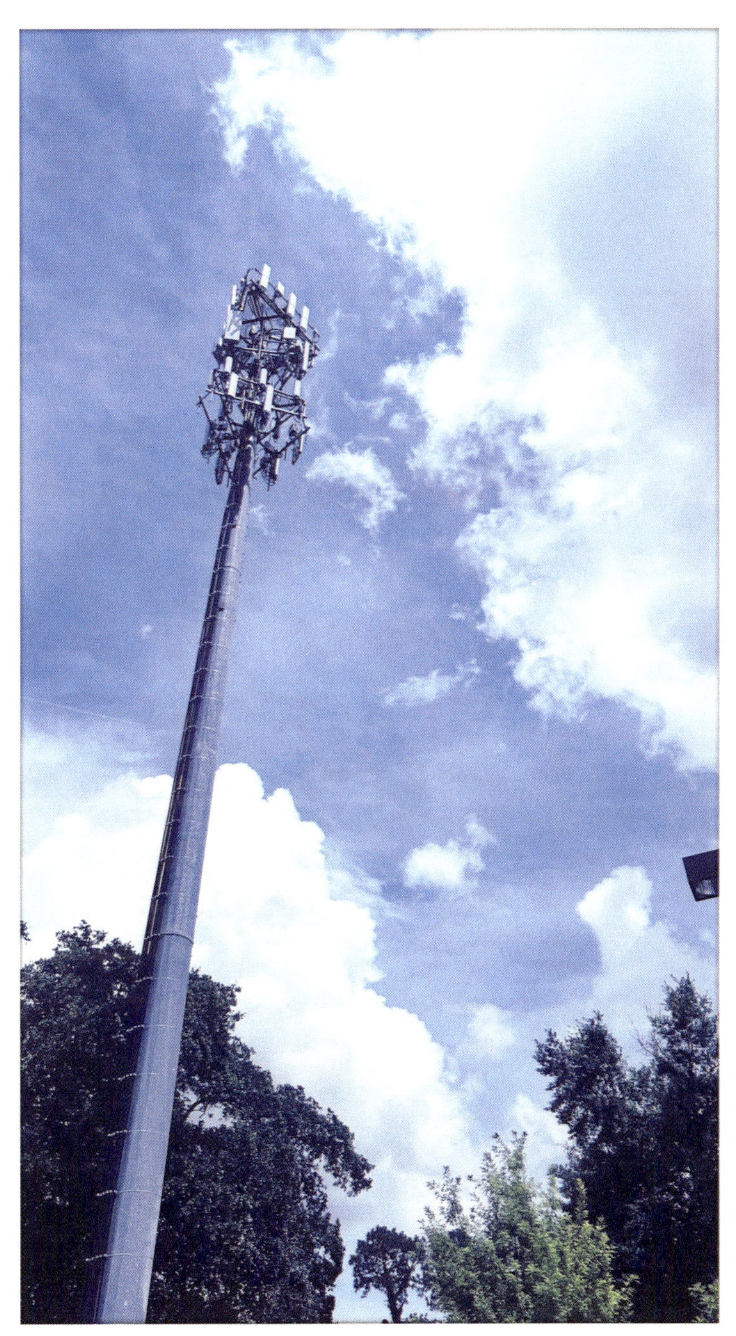

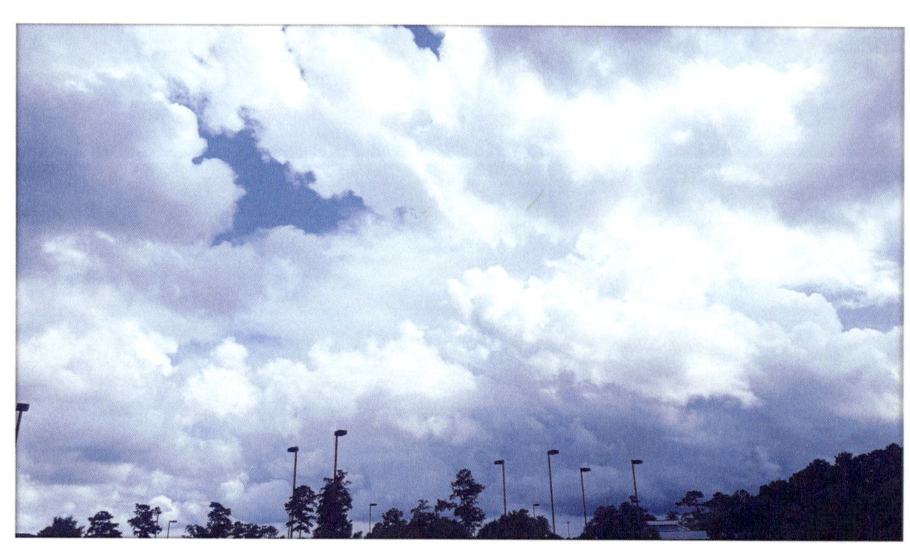

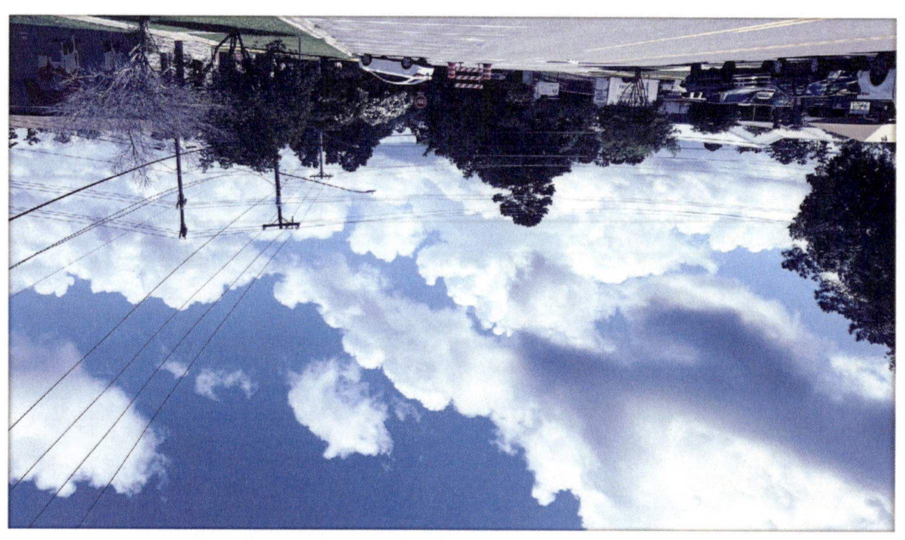

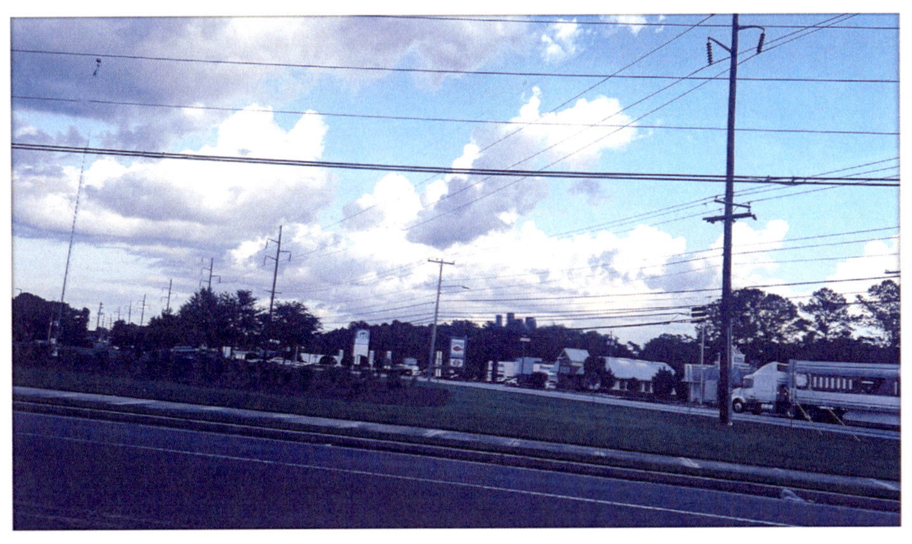

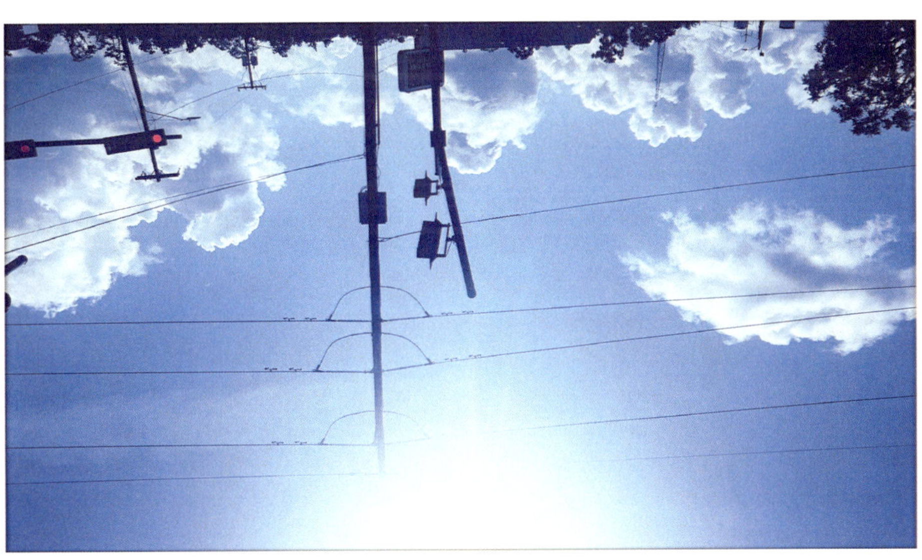

cloudform

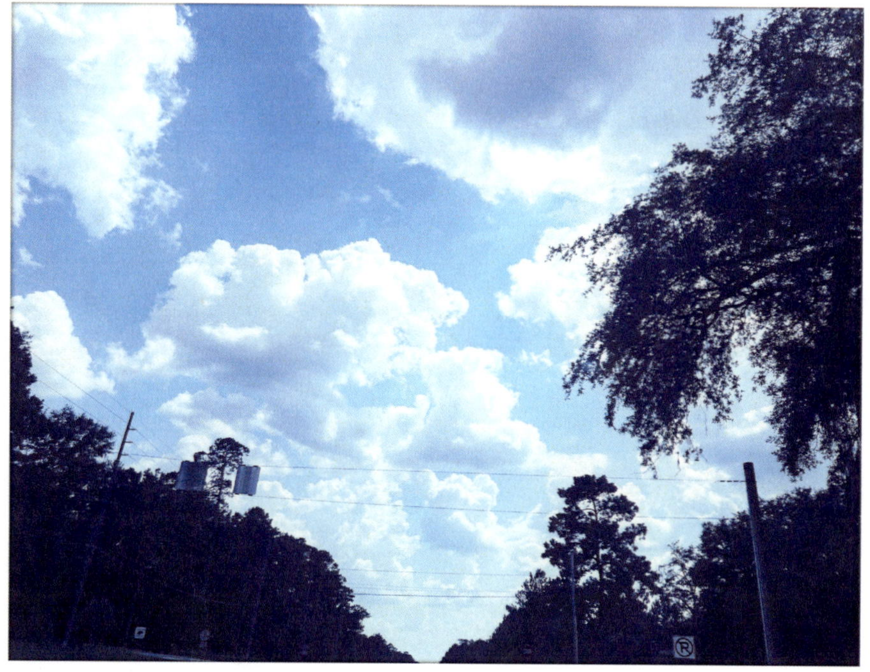

Jay Snodgrass is poet and artist living in Tallahassee, FL.

ChatGPT 4o is a large language model. Its operation is based on the GPT (Generative Pre-trained Transformer) architecture and is trained on vast amounts of text data so as to generate human-like text outputs.

hystericalbooks.com
2025

9 780940 821279